Jumping the Track

how abruptly changing directions
energized my life's calling

Roger Fields

Published by Blitz Ministries, Inc.
5028 Ashgrove Road,
Nicholasville, Kentucky 40356

ISBN 978-0-615-55732-8

Dedicated to

My wife, **Tammie Fields**
who jumped the tracks with me and
helped make Kidz Blitz a reality

Special thanks to

Tom and **Clara Fields**
my parents who supported
my track jumping

Terra Harrison and **Ande Long**
for their valuable input and never
being afraid to tell me the truth

Ken Dovey
for believing in this ministry from the
beginning and providing creative ideas

Jumping the Track

contents

INTRODUCTION

By an act of faith, Abraham said yes to God's call to travel to an UNKNOWN PLACE that would become his home. When he left he had no idea where he was going.

(Hebrews 11:8 The Message Bible)

Going...Somewhere

My life has been an adventure of going somewhere without knowing exactly where, letting God's plans override my own plans. Deciding to make abrupt changes in direction at strategic moments allowed me to live an exploratory life filled with wonder.

Life with the Lord has been like a remarkable road trip. I've experienced unexpected twists and turns in a journey as intriguing as the destination. I had big, exciting plans for my life; it turns out His plans were better.

I discovered that preparing myself for the path was more strategic than preparing the path itself. Instead of mapping out an exact plan to reach long term goals, I lived my life in a direction of God's leading while always alert to His next open door.

In other words, I don't target a specific destination. I put myself in situations that force me to develop personally/spiritually while leaving open options for whatever God has in mind. It has been more fulfilling to let God unfold new directions than to stick to a prescribed path at all costs. I don't compromise core values, but I am always open for a disruptive change in direction.

I call it "Jumping the Track."

My journey is not tidy. I made a few/many mistakes. There were lots of dark, discouraging times and things I would do differently now. But jumping the track is a powerful way of approaching life that adds wonder and energy. I hope that comes through.

God can do anything, you know—FAR MORE THAN YOU COULD EVER IMAGINE OR GUESS or request in your wildest dreams! He does it not by pushing us around but by working within us, his Spirit deep and gently within us.
(Ephesians 3:20 The Message Bible)

Think back to when you were a child
Your soul was free, your heart ran wild
Each day was different and life was a thrill
You knew tomorrow would be better still

Things have changed, you're much older now
You're unhappy and you don't know how
Why don't you look into Jesus, He's got the answer

Larry Norman

Jumping
the Track

Trust in the Lord with all your heart;

do not depend on your OWN UNDERSTANDING.

Seek his will in all you do,

and he will show you WHICH PATH TO TAKE.

(Proverbs 3:5,6 NLT)

Leave Me Alone

Here's my journey. It is a hodgepodge of seemingly random happenings that God wove together in a way that worked out better than I would have thought.

Hodgepodge

I am insecure, intensely shy and way too opinionated. At best, I am a mediocre husband and parent. Relationships are elusive to me. I am more comfortable being by myself than with people. I learned early in life that I am highly capable of saying the wrong thing at the wrong time in a group setting. I cope with my personality deficiencies by avoiding groups and keeping my mouth shut as much as possible.

> **"I may not have gone where I intended to go, but I think I have ended up where I needed to be."**
> --Douglas Adams

I try to be a leader and like to be thought of as a leader, but I am not one. There is nothing about me that lends itself to someone God would choose to work through.

So when Tammie, my wife, and I started Kidz Blitz Ministries in 1996, no one thought this type of high-energy family event would succeed. No one said, "Wow! That's a great idea, Roger!" The typical response was, "Hmm. Well, OK. That's interesting." No one flat out said I was a complete moron for trying something like this, but their lack of encouragement and body language spoke volumes. I got a lot of blank stares from friends, family and fellow ministers.

> **"Every happening, great and small, is a parable whereby God speaks to us, and the art of life is to get the message."**
> --Malcolm Muggeridge

My extended family thought I was looney. I spent every family reunion answering this question from various relatives: "Now, what is it you do?" I tried to explain Kidz Blitz the best I could. Later they would ask again, "Now, what is it you do?"

The early days of Kidz Blitz were rough/discouraging/depressing. We had no church backing, no company backing and very little encouragement from any ministry. No one thought Kidz Blitz was a good idea. Nobody got it. No one seemed to grasp the potential of what would happen if families came together and enjoyed a high-energy experience that could build their faith.

I was familiar with high-energy, evangelistic youth rallies such as Acquire the Fire, but I had never seen a high-energy event that could engage parents and their kids together. I was hoping that this thing I was creating, Kidz Blitz, was original, one-of-a-kind. I was convinced that any day soon I would stumble across a super-cool, family event that was already being done bigger and better than what I ever could. I really could not fathom that what I was trying to do wasn't already out there.

Was Kidz Blitz truly original? As weeks, months, miles rolled by, it became clear — Kidz Blitz is something unique.

I became committed, more like obsessed, with making Kidz Blitz Live the ultimate shared family experience. I tried everything. Every kind of game, special effect and prop. I spent hours and hours roaming the aisles at Home Depot and Lowe's to see if anything brightly colored and big triggered an idea. (In the Kidz Blitz version of the Bible, God made PVC pipe on the 8th day of creation.) I tried some things that worked. I tried lots of stuff that didn't work.

When I look back today, I shudder to think about the risk we took. Four young girls. No reliable income. No money in the bank. And no home. I'm not sure I could do it again.

I deeply regret I did not keep a diary. Why didn't I? I suppose because deep down I didn't believe Kidz Blitz would survive. The plan was far from perfect. But we took action. And didn't quit when quitting seemed to be the best option.

It was a bumpy road. Some good. Some bad. Some joyful. Some painful. All of it real.

Invisible

In a room full of people, my tendency is to blend in, be invisible. I was like that all through my life.

I wasn't a loner. I played on the playground with the other kids but never took the lead in anything and seldom talked to anyone. I didn't want to be the captain of the team, but I did want to play. I wasn't a nerd. Nerds made A's and played chess; I made C's and played checkers. I was just a shy kid who was comfortable being a shy kid.

Saying that I have never liked being the center of attention is an understatement. I am more of the invisible, fade into the wall kind of guy. Mostly I have liked that. I have always wanted to observe life, not participate on any meaningful level.

So, if you were God, what kind of ministry would you place me in...

- Christian book editor?
- Hospital chaplain?
- Bible college professor?

God chose none of the above. He put me in front of large crowds where I was the center of attention. I could no longer afford the comfort of being a spectator. I had to be a fully engaged participant, out front for all to see.

Lost Bullwinkle

I had just turned six when my mother dressed me in a Bullwinkle costume and sent me out on Trick or Treat night with a pint-sized gang of super-heroes and our adult neighbor, Mr. Mike.

Having just moved to a new neighborhood, I was in unfamiliar territory. It was nearly impossible to see out of the narrow eye holes in my cheap, plastic Bullwinkle mask. On top of that, we later learned that my near-sighted vision was so bad I couldn't see my house from our front yard. And it was dark!

So when I took a wrong turn off of a front porch after bagging some candy, my super-hero friends and I went our separate ways. Mr. Mike evidently failed to notice he was short one Bullwinkle.

I was a six-year old, blind Bullwinkle wondering around in an unfamiliar neighborhood looking for my house.

Some of the houses in my neighborhood had sunken driveways. The yards were about six feet higher than the driveways with steps leading up to the front door. That works fine unless it's dark on Halloween night and you're a blind Bullwinkle; then it's a problem. Come to find out when you run across a front yard at night without noticing the sunken driveway, you go air born. I became a flying Bullwinkle, that is, for a moment until I came crashing down onto the blacktop.

Now, I was not only a lost, blind Bullwinkle, but I was also dazed. When a blind, dazed Bullwinkle comes to your door for candy and you notice he is not all there, you should give him whatever he wants. People did. I was making a haul, but I was still lost.

I didn't seem to have it in me to stop someone and ask for help. I didn't even mention to people who were putting candy in my plastic pumpkin, "Hey, by the way, I am totally lost and have no idea where I am." Not wanting to be a bother to anyone, I just kept walking, looking for something familiar and collecting candy from the neighbors.

After circling the neighborhood a few times, I did what any lost, six-year old Bullwinkle would do. I knelt on the sidewalk and presented my eloquent prayer request to God: "Help this Bullwinkle get home."

He did. I don't remember how, but I finally got home. This was the first time I experienced what it meant to be out of the protective bubble of home. I was beginning to realized how involved I was in this thing called life.

Participation

I was learning that participation is woven into the fabric of life. From the get-go God arranged things so that people would have to participate in the adventure of life. Once born into this world you are—by default—a participant. No one is born a spectator. No one is allowed to merely observe life. You participate whether you like it or not. There are no bleachers. There are no monitors. Nobody sits on the bench. In life, no one gets to sit in the audience.

That was a hard lesson for someone like me who was more comfortable behind life's curtain. But there's even more. God can do anything He chooses, and He chooses to work through people, particularly those who aren't cemented their own agenda, their own detailed plan.

God designed it like this from the beginning. God did not create Adam and Eve to observe the Garden of Eden but to live in it and to tend it. Adam didn't even have the luxury of merely observing the animals. God gave him the job of naming them. Couldn't angels take care of the garden? Yes, but they didn't. Couldn't God have labeled the animals? Sure. But He didn't. Adam participated with God's creation from the moment he arrived. No instruction classes. No break-in period. Immediately, God placed him in the middle of the action. Eve joins in. Satan comes along. Kids are born. The human race is in full swing. And everybody is a player.

The Bible is a catalog of how God chooses to work in participation with ordinary people to achieve His purpose. He seldom did anything in the Bible without an individual or group partnering with Him.

Think about it.

Did He really need Moses to part the Red Sea and march the Israelites out of Egypt and away from Pharaoh? God could have transported them out of Egypt any way He chose. But He chose to use Moses. That's what the burning bush story is all about. God wanted a participant. He didn't NEED Moses and his sidekick, Aaron.

Did He really need David to kill Goliath? God could have given Goliath a sudden heart attack. He didn't NEED David and his two-bit slingshot.

Did God really need Noah to build a floating, three-story warehouse to save life on Earth. He could have sent everyone/everything to the highest peak and flooded the rest. He didn't NEED Noah and his boat.

Did God really need Peter to mosey over to Cornelius' house to tell him about Jesus? The angel told Cornelius that Peter was coming. Why couldn't the angel go ahead and tell Cornelius the gospel? Would that have really been so hard for the angel? But God put Cornelius and Peter together so Peter could tell Cornelius about Jesus.

And the list goes on.

God could do it all by Himself. Instead, He goes to extreme lengths to involve people. He wants people to participate with Him. Participation is in God's DNA. It took me a while to understand the ramifications of that.

Square Dancing in the Gym

I kept trying to hit the "opt out" button. And I managed to have a few small "victories" where I was able to temporarily squirm out of participating in life. This one almost got me killed.

The unconfirmed rumor was that Coach Wesley, my sophomore gym teacher, once played for the Pittsburgh Steelers. He was so muscular, so intimidating that we never asked him about his past. We were flat out afraid of him.

Whatever he said to do, we did. No questions. No hesitation. We just did it. Coach Wesley was not to be trifled with. So when he announced that we would spend the next week square dancing with the girls P.E. class, we complied. Better to square dance with the girls than be verbally berated in the locker room by Coach Wesley.

He paired us up. My partner was...not my type. She was three times my size and loud. I was at the peak of my shyness and a mere 140 pounds. She embarrassed me to the max. She slung me around, laughed incessantly and had the time of her life. I had a decision to make.

I could endure this abuse, or I could refuse to dance with Miss Sumo Wrestler and risk being killed by Coach Wesley. I couldn't take it anymore, I had to solve this.

Only days earlier Coach Wesley lit into me for being the last one to get onto the trampoline. I didn't raise my hand to get on until all the other kids took a turn. He chewed me out in front of the other students for not being more aggressive, for waiting until the end. So I had no interest in stirring up his wrath toward me again. But this square dancing fiasco had to stop. I decided that day there were things worse than Coach Wesley's anger.

When the music finally stopped, my partner and I were standing within 20-30 feet from the locker room door. This was my chance. With no explanation or warning, I marched off the gym floor and into the locker room. I never looked back.

I can still hear her yelling at the top of her lungs, "He was right here! Right here! And he left me! He just left me!" I kept walking...sweating...slightly trembling...but never looking back.

I got my books from the locker room and headed into the hallway. To this day I don't know why Coach Wesley didn't come after me. He never said a word about it.

This was a rare time when I successfully opted out. It was a personal victory.

I Just Sat There

Another time when I tried the "opt out" button, it didn't work out so well.

We had an evangelist come to our church. He specialized in reaching teenagers. Translation: he was very good at making us all feel guilty.

At the end of his message, he made an emotional appeal to all the teenagers to commit to reading their Bibles daily. It was very dramatic.

My section of about fifty kids responded. They ALL went up front and dedicated themselves to reading the Bible daily.

I just sat there. I didn't go forward because I didn't want to be noticed, but I ended up being the only one left in my section. The rest of the church was looking at me probably wondering why I didn't follow the rest of the kids. I sat by myself in a section that just vacated to the front. No one was left on my row or several other rows in front of me or behind me. Awkward. By not going up front, I became more conspicuous than if I had.

To this day I am not sure why I didn't follow my friends. I just didn't want to. It was probably a weird combination of intense shyness and stubborn independence, but one thing is certain: I didn't want to participate. By that time in my life I actually enjoyed reading my Bible. I had no theological problem with committing to reading it. But I was the only one in my youth group who wouldn't publicly commit. I just sat there still trying to find ways to opt out of participating in life. But by sitting alone with everyone looking at me, this one backfired. Nice try, Roger.

30 years later...

I pulled off highway I-64 East and into a random gas station. After filling up the tank of my Toyota Sequoia, I made my way into the quick stop store. I live on energy drinks and protein bars from gas stations. Not good, I know.

I wondered what this store would have to eat. After traveling about a half-million road miles, I have found that about 90% of everything in these stores is the same. But 10% is unique to each store. That's the part that interests me. What might this store have to eat that I don't normally see on the road?

As I was about to enter the store, an image flashed through my head. Suddenly, I knew what was in this store already. I knew where things were located. I knew the restrooms were on the left. I knew they sold hats by the door. I knew they had a large glass case in the middle of the store to display trinkets. I knew the ice cream freezer was located on the right. I could see the store interior in my head. I walked in, and it was laid out just as I had remembered. I had been there before. I couldn't remember pulling off that exit or going into that gas station, but I had.

This scene repeats itself over and over. I have traveled so much that I have the interior layout of scores of quick marts memorized without realizing it.

But here is what surprises me.

I am headed to yet another church where I will direct an event on stage in front of hundreds, maybe thousands. For 90 minutes I will be on center stage selecting kids and parents to do

22

something I have avoided most of my life: participation. They will participate in games/challenges designed to illustrate Bible principles.

In fifteen years I have travelled enough miles to circle the globe twenty times conducting events for hundreds of thousands. In forty denominations, over 50,000 people have made first time confessions of faith in Jesus.

How did this happen?

Really, how?

How did this happen to a kid too shy to ask for directions on Halloween, too backward to square dance in the gym, too intimidated to follow his youth group up front?

How did it come about that I now direct thousands to do what I never liked doing? How did this become my ministry…my life?

It was not planned. It was never my goal. I would never have chosen to pursue something like this. It is counter to the way I thought I was wired. But somehow, it is as if I was put on this planet to do this. How DID this happen?

Goals Gone Bad

Allowing God to put me in strategic situations caused doors to open, doors that would have remained closed if I had put my energy into planning my path in life.

For me, long term goal setting is the best way to miss open doors. When I am focused on MY long term goal, I can't pivot in new directions. That's why I don't set those type of goals. They say I should, but I don't. Not because I am lazy, but because I flat out don't believe that setting long term goals is the best way to move through life. I don't like having my own self-centered agenda, but I do like putting myself in places that provide options.

Setting long term goals limits my ability to respond to God. They hem me in. I have more confidence in God's leading than I have in my goal-setting. I would rather listen to God and let Him lead me so I can pivot in a new direction when He opens up new opportunities. I don't like to close my options.

Short term goals are helpful. Losing 20 pounds by Christmas. Getting out of debt in 3 years. Finishing the rough draft of this book while staying in a monastery in Ontario. Short-term goals give me focus. Long-term goals can limit me.

It's easy for Christian leaders to adopt the world's methods, but it is a bit weak for us to borrow practices from corporate America and use them to set our direction. Leadership/managerial books teach goal setting. Businesses set goals, make projections. That's not for me. I didn't want to pursue my "own plans" thinking they are God's.

> **What you ought to say is, "If the Lord wants us to, we will live and do this or that." Otherwise you are boasting about YOUR OWN PLANS, and all such boasting is evil.** (James 4:15-16 NLT)

No interpretation needed.

I want to be like a basketball player with the ball. Basketball players plant one foot—pivot foot—and move the other one. This allows them to be able to dart in any direction that opens up. The player becomes a triple threat. He can shoot, dribble or pass. His options are open. If his plan was simply to dribble down the court and attempt a lay up regardless of the changing defense, he would be stopped. It is his ability to quickly change directions that makes him a threat.

Some people set rigid, long term goals that provide no room

for God to open up new opportunities. They can't pivot toward those opportunities. They are on a path that cannot be altered. That's fine if: you are sure God has no other opportunities for you, that the world never changes or you have such a need for routine that change freaks you out.

I would rather focus on what God is doing than on working my plan. God's plan is always more fulfilling than my long term plans. I relentlessly follow His leading and put the pressure on Him. He can handle it.

> *I know your deeds. See, I have placed before you an OPEN DOOR that no one can shut.* (Revelation 3:8a NKJV)

I don't think following God and responding to God's open doors is meant to be tricky. When we set aside our plans, God opens doors. Our part is to keep our agenda out of the way and pay attention to what He is doing. Normally, we get consumed with our own plans and never recognize the doors God opens before us. That's what makes life dull, routine and predictable. Our own plans just aren't that interesting compared to what God wants to lead us into.

Did Moses set a long-term plan to get the Israelites out of Egypt? No, God showed up and led Moses to confront Pharaoh and lead His people out of there.

Did Peter have a long term plan to lead 3000 people to put their faith in Jesus? No, Jesus called him to be a fisher of men. If Peter had any long term plans, they would have included starting a Fish n" Chips along the shores of Galilee.

Can you imagine Paul, the apostle, setting long-term goals? Imagine him saying, "Within 5 years we plan to reduce Roman flogging by 20%, start 12 churches and ban stoning from the Roman Empire." He never spelled out any specific goals.

God's Spirit led him. Door opened. Paul pivoted.

Paul pushed ahead based on his calling from God, not his own goals. He wasn't lazy or nonchalant about his mission. The "one thing" he did was to always look ahead.

> **Brothers and sisters, I do not consider myself yet to have taken hold of it. But one thing I do: Forgetting what is behind and straining toward what is ahead, I press on toward the goal to win the prize for which God has called me heavenward in Christ Jesus.** (Philippians 3:13-14 NIV)

Paul's "goal" was not a specific achievement but a desire to live up to his individual calling in Christ. That's a goal I can run with. It's one that allows me to pivot when God opens a door.

And that's all I have ever wanted to do.

Someone recently asked me, "Roger, where do you see yourself in five years?" After a few seconds of deep contemplation and inner reflection, I shrugged and said, "I don't know."

I don't do things that way. Never have.

The Clumsy Art of Track Jumping

Mary: The Ultimate Track Jumper

Mary had plans. Her goal was to marry Joseph, settle down into a quiet life and have children. One visit from an angel changed all that. Gabriel told her that because she was "highly favored" of God, the Holy Spirit was going to overshadow her so she would get pregnant with the Son of God, thereby messing up all her plans. Quite a jolt for a teenage Jewish girl engaged to be married.

Mary was undoubtedly on a track. Like other young Jewish girls she saw herself settling into a traditional Jewish life with her new husband, Joseph. She probably envisioned a quiet home where Joseph would support them through his carpenter work as they raised a family. Who knows, she may have had dreams of starting a Homemakers Society in her neighborhood for youg Jewish mothers.

Then Gabriel showed up without warning and suddenly announced a new track. Mary could have resisted saying, "No way am I going to face my family and friends pregnant and try

SET JUMP GOALS TRACK	
long term goals	unpredictable track
safe	risky
career	adventure
stay on course	open up options
routine	journey
ho hum	wow!
predictable	surprises
smart	crazy
normal	quirky
small success	big failures/successes
small lessons	big lessons
pays well	fulfilling
looks good	jaw dropping
enjoyable	breath-taking
manage	lead
improve	invent
measureable	immeasurable
smooth	abrupt
same old thing	constant change
job	passion
meet expectations	go wild

to convince them that God is the one who did this!" She could have fought to stay on the track she was on. Not wanting Jesus to be born to a disgruntled woman, God may have honored Mary's objection. But Mary didn't object. She was willing to give up her own plans, jump the track and follow God into a life she could never have imagined.

Listen to what she said.

Then Mary said, "Behold the maidservant of the Lord! LET IT BE TO ME ACCORDING TO YOUR WORD." And the angel departed from her. (Luke 1:38 NKJV) In today's vernacular that translates into, "Let's do it!"

Then everything changed. She found herself in a barn with a new baby as shepherds showed up telling her what the angels said in the field: that Jesus was their Savior. Two years later kings showed up at the house bringing expensive gifts. Then Herod killed all the baby boys trying to destroy Jesus. Mary's life was not what she planned, but it became an adventure from God that forever changed history.

Mary is the ultimate track jumper.

Right Track?

The most important question I ever asked myself is this: Am I on the right track?

For me, life is not about setting and achieving a personal goal, but about keeping my eyes open so I can change directions based on God's leading and new information. It is about leaving what is predictable to pursue what is unpredictable, leaving what is normal and expected to pursue what is unique and unexpected. It is about abruptly leaving a path that is comfortable and going down a new path that is frightening.

My track, not my goals, determines my destination. Anyone can have goals, ambitions, dreams and desires. But the most important question anyone can ask themselves is the one I mentioned: Am I on the right track? Ultimately, our track is what takes us to our destination. I can have a goal to be a doctor, but if I am not on a track that leads to

A leader is the one who climbs the tallest tree, surveys the entire situation, and yells: 'Wrong jungle!"
--Steven Covey

medical school, I won't reach my destination. Track trumps goals.

Staying on track to reach a destination is only as powerful as the destination itself. When God opens a new door toward a better destination, my willingness to abruptly change directions makes all the difference in my journey and where I end up...so far. Following His destination sometimes means leaving the standard way of doing things. It may mean being unconventional and far less normal. It means understanding that God has a unique path for me and that following that path may require an uncomfortable change in trajectory.

That's jumping the track.

The default method is to allow the expectations of my peers to influence my goals and, therefore, influence my direction. Most ministers tend to aspire to pastor a large church one day. Why? Because that's what their peers expect and value. They are expected to move toward that goal, not because it's a goal God set for them but because it's the goal that's valued among their ministry friends. I was no different.

Setting a long term goal based on the expectations of others would have guaranteed that I missed my destiny. Following the track toward goals others expected from me, I would have...

1. Failed to recognize open doors from God because they didn't meet my long term plan.

2. Ended up frustrated at my inability to meet the goal that was never designed for me in the first place. Or even worse, I might have met the goal only to discover it wasn't worth my life.

3. Missed the thrill of jumping the track and going in a direction that wasn't already defined in my head.

Shattering the expectations of others is what I had to deal with when I entered children's ministry. I had already served as a lead pastor. I was still deeply involved in adult ministry when I later became an associate minister at a large church.

Track Jumping Questions I Ask Myself

1. Can I abandon my plan if I realize it takes me where I don't want to go?

2. Will I stop doing something that is not working?

3. Is there an open door I am missing?

4. Do I care too much about my status?

5. Am I ready to change?

6. Have I become too complacent?

7. Am I living by faith or fear?

8. Have I learned anything lately?

9. Am I too normal?

10. Am I paying attention to God's leading?

So entering children's ministry after serving in adult ministry surprised my minister friends. Most step from children's ministry to associate minister to lead pastor. That was the expected track. I jumped the track.

No minister I knew had ever done this. There was no pattern to look at and learn from. I was a train cutting my own path across the prairie. And that is the part of it I loved!

I wasn't moving toward an arbitrary goal set by myself or the expectations of others. I was moving full steam in a direction God set for me with no idea where it was all going to end up. That thrill was my spiritual adrenaline rush, the exhilaration of watching something unfold that I didn't micromanage. I feel sorry for people who settle for marching toward a pre planned goal that merely reflects what others expect you to do.

> **"Great leaders are effective, not because they have all the answers, but because they have a tenacity to act."**
> --Michael Hyatt

Today, I am constantly surprised at what God has done through Kidz Blitz. It is deeply fulfilling to see how God has impacted kids, families and churches. I am grateful that He has abundantly provided for my family through this ministry. I know it is not because of my ability or creativity that all this has happened. I also know that none of it was realized because I set a long term goal and set out to make it happen.

I have traded predictability for wonder and adventure. I don't have the luxury of lying in bed with the assurance that my life is mapped out, but instead I lie in bed wondering what new ideas, direction or solutions tomorrow might bring. Predictability was a casualty when I jumped the track. I had to learn to live without it.

Have you ever jumped the track to do what God was leading you to do? Have you ever veered way off the path? If you haven't, you might want to try it. It's not for everybody, but I recommend it. That is if you don't mind having the &%$# scared out of you.

> *Keep your eyes open, hold tight to your convictions, give it all you've got, be resolute, and love without stopping.* (1 Corinthians 16:13,14 MSG)

Track Jumpers in the Bible

The Bible is full of track jumpers. Think about it. Every renegade of faith in the Bible left the prescribed path and raced ahead in an unplanned direction. They realized they were in the "wrong jungle."

No one planned for Moses to beat down Pharaoh and spring a million Jews from Egypt. His track was to grow up as a dignitary in Egypt. No one planned for childless Abraham to relocate and get on the nation-starting track. No one planned for Peter to leave the fishing industry track and influence a spiritual movement that would span the globe. The list goes on.

Here are three of my favorite track jumpers from the Bible.

Paul

Paul was firmly on the Jewish track. He was a respected Jewish Pharisee (Philippians 3:5) whose ministry led him, not to Jews, but to Gentiles. His life experience suggested he should reach Jews with the Gospel. God had other plans.

> *I have set you as a LIGHT to the GENTILES, that you should be for salvation to the ends of the earth.* (Acts 13:47 NKJV)

Paul jumped track and began starting churches made up

mostly of non-Jews. No church today would have suggested someone like Paul should reach out to the people most opposite to himself.

David

David's track was tending sheep. That was his job, his responsibility, his life. The back story of his defeat of Goliath is not that a boy killed a giant, but that a kid jumped the track of what he was expected to do and did what was unexpected. You can hear the disgust coming from his brothers as they tried to get him to return to his old track.

> *Now Eliab his oldest brother heard when he spoke to the men; and Eliab's anger was aroused against David, and he said, "Why did you come down here? And with whom have you LEFT THOSE FEW SHEEP in the wilderness? I know your pride and the insolence of your heart, for you have come down to see the battle."* (1 Samuel 17:28 NKJV)

His big brother couldn't handle the fact that David was jumping the track. Sheep tending was his track, not giant killing. Eliab was trying to get David back on track by asking him who was taking care of the sheep. Eliab didn't care about "those few sheep." He was offended that David wouldn't stay on his track.

By jumping the track, God was able to place him on his new track of becoming king. His destination changed from one day becoming a first class sheep herder to becoming the king of Israel.

Jesus

Even Jesus was a track jumper. According to His friends and family, He was supposed to stay on the carpenter track. His track was making furniture.

And when the Sabbath had come, He began to teach in the synagogue. And many hearing Him were astonished, saying, "Where did this Man get these things? And what wisdom is this which is given to Him, that such mighty works are performed by His hands! IS THIS NOT THE CARPENTER, the Son of Mary, and brother of James, Joses, Judas, and Simon? And are not His sisters here with us?" So they were offended at Him. (Mark 6:2,3 NKJV)

Those around Jesus couldn't get their arms around the fact that Jesus jumped from making furniture to making disciples. That wasn't supposed to happen. For them, He was the local carpenter, not the world's Savior. The big difference with Jesus is that He knew from the beginning He was going to jump tracks. He knew why He came to earth. We don't live with the same clarity, but even still, Jesus demonstrates what it means to jump the track.

A Bias for Action

Sometimes God's direction is not crystal clear. Sometimes there's a choice to make and I'm not sure which way to go. It could be God doesn't care because He knows He will work things out either way. Or it could be that the time is not right to make the choice. Sometimes I have to feel my way around until His direction becomes clear.

Action brings clarity. When I don't know what to do, I lean toward doing something, anything. I have a bias for action. We plan too much, think too much, meet too much and do too little. There is power in action.

I do what Samuel did when he was trying to find out which of Jesse's boys he was supposed to anoint as king. God could have made it clear, but He didn't. So instead of kicking back and waiting for God to spell it out, he took action. It is easier for God to direct a moving vessel than a stagnant one.

Samuel marched Jesse's boys out one at a time to figure out which one God wanted him to anoint as king. After each boy came out, God said in effect, "Nope, not that one." Finally, Samuel asked Jesse if he had any other boys. Jesse admitted he had one more but that he wasn't very impressive. He brought David in and God directed Samuel to anoint him. Samuel heard God say "no" several times before he heard Him say "yes."

That's exactly the way it works for me. If it seems as though God is leading me in a certain direction, I pursue that direction until I hear God say, "no." Then I back off and move in a different direction. If I keep moving, eventually I will get clarity from God.

Sometimes when I act God says, "Wait." I obey. I find it easier to hear God say "wait" than to hear Him say, "Get up and go do _____!" I am not a fan of plunging ahead when God is putting on the breaks, but I am less of a fan of putting God in the position of having to jump start me. Moving boats are easier to steer than the ones in the dock.

> **"I make a decision. If I make the wrong decision, then I make another one."**
> --Dave Ramsey

Is that an Old Testament method only? I don't think so. Paul did the same thing in Acts. Jesus called Paul to bring the Gospel to the Gentiles, so Paul was trying to figure where to go to do the job. He wanted to know where his next missionary gig would be.

Now when they had gone through Phrygia and the region of Galatia, they were FORBIDDEN by the Holy

Spirit to preach the word in Asia. After they had come to Mysia, they tried to go into Bithynia, but the Spirit did NOT PERMIT them. So passing by Mysia, they came down to Troas. And a vision appeared to Paul in the night. A man of Macedonia stood and pleaded with him, saying, "Come over to Macedonia and help us." Now after he had seen the vision, immediately we sought to go to Macedonia, concluding that the Lord had called us to preach the gospel to them. (Acts 16:6-19 NKJV)

Paul kept moving (groping) as God kept stopping him. Then… he got clarity to go to Macedonia. Clarity came AFTER action. That's the way it works for me. Action first, then clear direction. I can't sit around and expect God to show me my next step. I move, He shows. There is no substitute for action.

Energized

Whatever I do in life, whatever course I pursue, I know I need one thing in abundance: energy. I know I can never get anywhere unless I am energized to do what God has called me to do. If I am going to take action, I need energy. Lots of energy!

I know that I cannot be energized unless I am on a track that invigorates me. A boring track means no energy to move down the track. I have realized along the way that I do not have the capacity to stay energized on a track I don't believe in.

Lots of people get burned out not because they work too hard, but because their track no longer energizes them. I can work long hours and not feel fatigued if my track is exciting to me. However, a few hours of hard work in a direction that no longer captures my imagination can cause me to feel exhausted. I have to get up in the morning energized about my day.

That has become a key indicator for me as to whether or not I am on the right road. I ask this question of myself: "Am I excited to be doing what I am doing?" If not, why? Could I be on the wrong track? I am unwilling to spend my life doing something that doesn't get me up in the morning with anticipation about the day. With energy, I am a force. Without it, I am a dud.

3 Types

There are three ways I could choose to go through life. The first two are common. The last one is scarce.

1. Flounderers. This is the person who goes through life with no direction, no goals, no vision. They have no drive and no curiosity. Flounderers can't see beyond today. They never seem to have a purpose in life. They are cynical and self-absorbed ending up needy and dependent on other people. They live for the moment to the point that they never go anywhere in life. Sadly, this represents the majority of people.

2. Goal Setters. This person has a goal and is determined to reach it at all costs. They have drive but little curiosity. Nothing else matters. They will work and sacrifice to reach their goal. Their goal might be anything: becoming a doctor, owning a business, getting a promotion, owning a house on the beach, etc. Goal setters have a plan and a purpose. They normally accomplish much. Sometimes they reach their goals only to discover they are still unhappy, unfulfilled and empty. They climbed to the top and realized not much was there.

3. Track Jumpers. These are the people who have direction and purpose, but who refuse to be shackled to any one goal. They have an abundance of drive and curiosity. They realize God may have better plans for them than they have for themselves. They move forward in a direction, and maybe even toward a specific goal. But they are distinct in that they always have their eyes open for a possible change in direction. They refuse to be married to their goals. Their commitment is more to following God's leading than in a specific achievement. For them, life is an ever-evolving adventure, full of wonder and amazement. This is the way I recommend living life.

Strengths

Prevailing wisdom says that you should play to your strengths, find out what you are good at and maximize it. To a point, there is wisdom in that. It is certainly best for an organization to have people in positions where their strengths can shine. You wouldn't want your music ministry running your nursery. Organizations progress largely on having the right people in the right places.

The problem, however, is when you limit someone to doing only what they are good at. You can end up with an effective worker dying on the inside because they cease to be challenged. They are on a track that uses their expertise but leaves them unfulfilled.

The music minister might be more personally energized by going into mission work. The church secretary might come alive if she is also allowed to serve in the youth group. But neither might be effective at first.

What's best for the organization short term is not always best for the individual. Some people are more alive when they leave a track that highlights their expertise for one that allows them to grow into their position.

Paul's strengths rested in his rich Jewish heritage, yet his calling in life was reaching non-Jews. He certainly didn't play to his strengths. His strength was Hebrew theology, something Gentiles couldn't care less about.

My strengths were not in children's ministry when God opened up the doors for me. I learned a big, exciting secret: I can develop! That's right. I may never be a world-class musician (or even city-class for that matter) or play in the NBA, but certain skills can be developed. Few things are as exciting to me than the deep conviction that I can learn just about anything. I refuse to limit myself with phrases like "well, I'm just not cut out for that." I know that we all have different spiritual gifts and not everyone can do everything. But I decided not to assume I can't do something if I never tried. Maybe I am gifted in that area, maybe I'm not, but if will never know if I don't jump in and give it a whirl.

Can you imagine Peter responding to Jesus with the attitude we use sometimes? "I'm sorry, Jesus. I just don't think I'm cut out to be a fisher of men." I refuse to limit myself. If my abilities limit me, fine. If my gifting limits me, fine. But I will not limit myself. If I have a passion to do something then I race ahead and find out if I am skilled/gifted at it. If I discover I am not up to the task, then I have just learned something very valuable about myself. I want to know what my strengths are and what they are not, what can be developed and what cannot be developed. And I can't know if I don't try.

Excellent Failure

I had to learn to redefine failure. For so long, I was afraid to try things because I was afraid to fail. I thought failure meant: I made a big, stupid mistake and should be punished. Then I realized that only cowards never fail because they never try anything. Failing didn't mean I was stupid; it meant I was brave enough to try something that might have worked.

"Reward excellent failures. Punish mediocre successes"
--Phil Daniels

Redefining failure as something positive gave me courage.

Anyone and everyone in history who ever did anything significant had one thing in common: lots of failure. They embraced failure, rather than feared it. The same is true with people of faith in the Bible. They ALL had significant failures.

I had to treat failure as a badge, not a scarlet letter. I had to be willing to say, "Yep! I planted a church in Tampa and it went nowhere." I may have failed, but I knew a hundred ministers that would never have even tried to move their family to Tampa and plant a church from scratch.

I had to "reward" myself for trying something big and be willing to "punish" myself when I lapsed into settling for mediocre success. Put another way, I had to feel good about myself for trying and failing at something that was worth trying. "Excellent failure" means it was worth the risk.

"Success is the ability to go from one failure to another with no loss of enthusiasm."
--Winston Churchill

"Mediocre success" means what I did worked but it was no big deal; the success was irrelevant because nobody cared that it worked.

I made a conscious, deliberate decision that I would rather fail at something that would have rattled the world than succeed at something that had no impact. That decision freed me from the fear of failure. Instead of imagining what happen if I failed, I imagined what would happen if I succeeded.

Big failure is more valuable than small success. I learn nothing from small, incremental successes. I learn and grow from trying something big, even when it fails. So even in the worst case, I will learn lessons worth gold. Big failures mean big lessons.

Becoming an Irritation

Anytime I decided to jump the track, people around me tried to discourage me. They reasoned that they wouldn't try something so bold, so why should I try? They were afraid of failure so I should be too. They felt obligated to try and stop me.

Victor, a longtime friend of mine, jumped tracks and gave his entire extended family a collective heart attack. Right out of college with an engineering degree, a large power plant hired him to supervise a dozen men much older than him. The pay was

> **"There's a war between people who are trying to do something and the people who are trying to keep them from doing something wrong."**
> --Tom Peters

great. His position commanded respect. He was doing what he went to school to do. But he hated it. After a few years of good pay and a miserable life, he jumped the track to do what he always wanted to do. He went back to school and became a nurse. Everyone tried to stop him except for his wife. She understood his frustration. He now oversees a group of nurses in a medical facility in Kentucky. And loves it.

There is another issue with those that frown on track jumping. They feel trapped in the one direction they have chosen and when they see you jump tracks it makes them envious. It reminds them that they settled for a life less fulfilling than they desire. Your courage lets them know they could do more with their life. And that bothers them. You threaten their belief that they have to stay on their current track. They want to believe they have no choice. You show them that they do have a choice.

Before You Jump the Track

Track jumping is NOT for everyone. I have a good friend who has spent his entire adult life working for the Department of Motor Vehicles. He is not about to jump tracks. He is safe and secure. He doesn't like his job but he would dislike change even more. He should probably stay put. That's OK.

Often when we hear success stories we lose vital details that explain what is was like to be there. We don't get a sense of the struggle, the surprises, the stress or the outright fear. I wrote this book to help give you a feel of what it was like when I jumped the track. Having jumped the track in significant ways five times, I wanted to give you, the reader, a sense of what it was like so that you could make an informed decision about your own life. You could either decide to stay on the track you are on or be ready and willing to jump tracks when the time is right.

For those not up for the unpredictable nature of track jumping, I want to scare you out of it. Don't do it! If you are content doing what you are doing; stay where you are. If stress freaks you out; stay where you are. If you value security more than significance; stay where you are. Consider yourself warned.

For those who aren't content to stay on the same track indefinitely, I want to provoke you to take bold action. If you fear living with regrets of not trying then I want to help you jump the track. You are the only one who can decide whether or not track jumping is right for you. If you decide to jump the track, I promise you one thing: there will be times when you will regret making the jump. Everything will not be smooth all the time.

You may go through it bloody and beaten, but in the end, you will realize it was your destiny.

here we go...

jumping **5**
DIFFERENT
kinds of tracks

1. **Shyness Track**
2. **Tradition Track**
3. **Settled Track**
4. **Honor Track**
5. **Status Quo Track**

My Jump List
Stuff I better be clear about in my own life

1. I am going to make mistakes. I better learn to get over it.
2. When I make the wrong decision, I can then make a new one.
3. Big changes in direction energize me more than small improvements.
4. People are everything.
5. Facing the truth about my own weaknesses helps me move ahead.
6. Taking action works better than thinking hard.
7. God is good at opening and shutting doors.
8. Eternity is more important than here and now.
9. God can do more in me, and through me, than anyone, including me, thinks is possible.
10. What people think of me does not control my life unless I let it.
11. Doing crazy things is more energizing than doing predictable things.
12. Doing is better than watching.
13. Goals get old. Following open doors from God doesn't.
14. I will not limit myself.
15. I might as well embrace constant change whether I like it or not.
16. Enjoying what I do in life is not an option for me.
17. Changing my direction has more impact than trying to change the world.
18. I can change my direction faster than I can change the world.
19. My track will take me to a destination. I need to make sure it is a good destination.
20. It never hurts anything to ask myself if I am on the right track.
21. Learning is a life long hobby.
22. Try new things I probably can't do.
23. There is always a better way of doing things.
24. It doesn't help anyone to get bogged down in doing things that don't matter.
25. My personal goals are too limiting for me.
26. When I make mistakes I will fix them fast.
27. God to be faithful to what He says in His word.
28. Tough decisions are necessary.
29. I won't say, "I'm not cut out for that."
30. It is great fun to push the limits of what can be done.
31. I can learn from the stupid things I do and from the stupid things other people do.
32. My journey is worth enjoying.
33. I will look for my next step forward.
34. Risk is a normal part of life.

Jumping the Shyness Track

stretching
my personality

People Are Over-Rated

My parents raised me well, to love and serve God. I have never known a broken home, an alcoholic father or abuse. I didn't realize how valuable that was until later in life. I was given every advantage.

But in spite of that, my life became a mix of churchy, religious ingredients that gave me the air of superiority and did nothing to build relationships. I became critical of everyone. The problem with being a perpetual critic is that you believe others are also critical. That happened to me. I assumed everyone was judging me, so I second-guessed my every word, my every action. I became even more shy than I already was by nature.

From 14-17 years old I worked for a civil engineering firm in Lexington. The garage/shop was my domain every day after school where I built core boxes. Civil engineers like to drill deep holes in the ground to see what's down there. That way contractors don't build big buildings, roads and dams on ground that might one day collapse. I can appreciate the wisdom in that. Apparently they need crates to haul off the samples of rock and dirt they drill out of the ground. That's where I came in. I built long wooden boxes with neat little sections and a hinged top. The job was perfect for me. I would work four or five days in a row and never see anyone. As long as I kept core boxes piled up for the taking, they were happy and I was happy. The company owners didn't bother me, and I didn't bother them. And since the general public doesn't feel compelled to walk in off the street to buy core boxes, I could happily work in seclusion for days at a time.

The only down side was that my shop was not air conditioned and located between to garbage dumpsters. So in the summer I left the doors open for a breeze while the fly population traveled back and forth between dumpsters through my sweat shop. It was just me and the flies. To this day I hate flies with a passion, due to that job. But except for the flies, it was the perfect job for me. Whistling away, I built core boxes for three years.

I was a good kid who liked feeling superior to others. It helped me cope with my inability to fit in. Anytime I felt down I could remind myself how ungodly most other people were. That comforted me. I didn't have much use for people.

I was over-churched and under-saved.

Being completely immersed in church gave me a group of friends to hang out with, camps to go to in the summer, and events to keep me busy. Church kept me from the "big sins" and taught me the books of the Bible. But it didn't make Jesus real to me.

Of the sixty plus kids in our church youth group, none of us had much to do with God in any personal way. Most of us were decent kids, we just didn't find God particularly interesting or relevant. Summer church camp and choir trips were cool. Everything else was hum drum. Everyone got along fairly well. Everyone, that is, except Kevin.

Kevin sold drugs. Kevin's family was active in the church so Kevin was too. He was a teenager when his family joined our church, and the boys in our youth group decided that we hated Kevin. His family was wealthier than ours. The girls liked him. And he was a drug pusher! We felt like he invaded our tight-knit, well-mannered, Christian club.

Kevin the Pusher went on our youth choir trip to the Midwest. We saw Oral Roberts University, the St. Louis Arch and some other boring stuff. Ironically, we spent the night at my future Bible college, Ozark Christian in Joplin, Missouri. That night,

Kevin slipped out of the dorm with two girls, got drunk and arrested. There was an article about it in the *Joplin Globe* the next day. He embarrassed everyone: the choir, the church, the college, our ministers.

Later that year we all went to summer camp. We put gross stuff in Kevin's sleeping bag and generally made his life hell. We knew God would be proud of us for punishing him.

Shortly after Kevin the Pusher turned sixteen, he got his license and had a crippling car accident. He was high and speeding. From my perspective, he deserved to wreck. Kevin broke lots of bones and had to be in the hospital for weeks. We never went to see him. We were glad he was away from us for a while. Good riddance.

OLD TRACK	NEW TRACK
inward	outward
in back	in front
principles	people
play it safe	take a risk
tolerate	care
tune out	listen
take	give

Kevin the Pusher got out of the hospital and started a Bible study. I was skeptical. Why would anyone, particularly Kevin, want to read the Bible? I had the impression that everything that happened in the Bible was for that time only, not for today. Why would anyone want to study it? I had never heard of anyone, particularly teens, going to someone's house to study the Bible. At this point in my life I had not yet started reading the Bible. It turns out that Kevin read the Bible for six weeks while he was laid up in the hospital. He was amazed by what was in it. So he started telling people what he was learning.

Kevin's Bible study caught fire. Every teenager I knew attended. Living rooms were packed. It grew bigger than the youth group. I was stunned. Trying to figure all this out, I bought a "reading" Bible. Let me be clear here. It isn't that I didn't own a Bible. My Bible was very pretty, but I needed one I could actually understand. I bought an NIV New Testament and started reading and underlining. It was a funny feeling the first time I wrote in my Bible. It always seemed wrong somehow. But Kevin said it was alright.

Kevin became my best friend. We listened to early Jesus music together and talked about the Bible. He stopped selling drugs, but while he never did them around me, I was aware that he sometimes fell into using them again. He joined the military when he graduated. I haven't seen him or talked to him since. People tell me he has had a hard life and continued to struggle with drugs. But I will always be grateful to him for turning me on to the Bible.

Kevin showed me that Jesus is more interesting than church. For the first time, Jesus seemed relevant to me.

Doing Something with My Life

After graduating from high school I spent three miserable semesters at the University of Kentucky studying computer science. That was my track. With my people skills it was a perfect fit. I could graduate, get a decent paying job and ride out my days in a back office with limited human interaction. Then it hit me. I didn't want that destination. If you could have handed me a college degree in computer science and given me a 100k job, I would have turned it down. My track was headed in the wrong direction, even though it made sense for someone like me. Hate is a strong word so let me say it this way: I HATED studying computer science.

One day I abruptly marched into my parent's living room and announced that I was leaving UK and enrolling in Bible college. I decided to move to Joplin, Missouri to attend Ozark

Christian College. A few weeks later I packed up my bass guitar and left my home in Lexington for the first time. I didn't know what I wanted in life, but I knew it wasn't computer science.

From computer science to ministry: this was my first experience at track jumping.

My first night in my Bible college dorm was a jolt. It was nothing I expected.

Back then our week day curfew was 9:00 unless you were in the library. Then you could stroll in at the wild and woolly hour of 9:30. Floor devotions started every night at 10:00.

So…expecting a high level of spirituality from my future preacher comrades, I entered the dorm at 9:30 from the library. I situated myself on the hallway floor waiting for a crowd of young men to gather. At 10:00 the only one to show up was a student wearing what appeared to be a World War II pilot's helmet and goggles. It was entertaining to look at but not what I expected from a future minister.

Over the next hour and a half, dozens of my college dorm mates began sneaking through windows and propped open doors. A handful showed up for devotions. My jaw dropped.

Our 80+ year old dorm mother, affectionately known as Mom K, had her work cut out for her. She spent her time roaming the halls looking for wayward boys. At four feet tall, she didn't appear menacing at first, but nothing intimidated her. She was fearless and relentless. We could out run her, but she knew where we lived.

This was not what I thought Bible college would be like. It was not what I thought ministers in training would be like. I expected straight laced, non-athletic, skinny geeks. What I found instead was Curt the Bear Wrestler, Scott the Weight

Lifting Champion, Steve the Hippie, Bruce the Black Belt, and an assortment of guys who had been kicked out at least once before. Again, I didn't fit in. Most of them were different than what I expected, so I had a hard time relating to them.

One thing about track jumping, the surprises never end.

Papa Funk

Larry Bryant is my lifelong friend. He was known in Bible college as Papa Funk because of his over-the-top musical ability. We grew up together attending the same schools and the same church, Southland Christian Church in Lexington, Kentucky. We were later Bible college roommates and best men in each other's weddings. Yet, he was a never ending source of irritation. Why? Because, he is loaded with more talent than anyone deserves. While I aspired to one day adequately play bass guitar, he could do anything musically. Anything.

Many nights I would crash early on my college room bed while Larry would sit at his desk playing it like a piano! Other musicians would give him songs on cassette tapes, and he would listen to the tunes and pretend his desk was a piano. He could hear the chords in his head as he wrote down the chord charts. Really. How many people can play a desk like a piano and hear the notes? Irritating.

Larry's gifted musical ability and magnetic personality always amazed those of us who knew him. Most nights I fell asleep with a deepening realization of how little talent I really had.

Larry formed a mock 60's band to perform at a special event at our college. "Lovely Larry and the Heartbeats" rocked the crowd. He asked me to be a backup singer, a role that didn't require recognizable talent. It was a cool opportunity to perform on stage in this music/comedy band he put together. However, I couldn't do it. I was too shy. The group only performed once, but Larry made everyone in the band famous on campus.

Ask me to do something simple/fun on stage and I panic. But if you need something rushed to the post office, I'm your man.

A big studio from Nashville contacted Larry one day and wanted to record one of his songs. It was a huge break for him. All he had to do was sign the release and overnight it back to the publisher. They had to have the release immediately or they wouldn't have time to include it on the album. Most musicians would have moved heaven and earth to get the release signed and returned immediately. Larry signed it, gave it to me to mail and announced his softball team had a game. He chose to play softball rather than make sure his song release made it to the publisher on time.

I mailed it. The song did well. Larry's musical career was off and running. He went on to write a string of top selling songs for the biggest Christian artists in America.

His softball career went nowhere.

In one of my classes Knofel Staton, one of the professors I admired, taught a lesson about the grace of God. It was a different kind of lesson than we normally heard at Bible college. It was about the fact Jesus' death, burial and resurrection is enough to completely pay for our salvation.

Larry was in the class. The lesson impacted him deeply. He wrote a song about grace. There were evidently others who needed clarification about the Gospel because "It Was Enough" went on to be a #1 Christian song recorded by Gary McSpadden.

That song stuck with me. I was beginning to get it. It's not about what we do for God. It is about what God did for us.

Larry captured the struggle all of us feel at one time or another, the struggle to please God and live up to what He wants us to be. Larry took criticism from people who felt the song made grace cheap. But it captured the power of the Gospel and helped shape the direction of my ministry years later.

LORD I SEE SO MUCH IN ME
THAT I JUST CAN'T GET RIGHT
THINGS THAT WEIGH ME DOWN EACH DAY
AND STEAL MY SLEEP AT NIGHT
IN YOUR WORD I READ ABOUT
A PEACE I WISH I FELT
BUT HOW CAN YOU FORGIVE ME WHEN
I CAN'T FORGIVE MYSELF

(CHORUS)
IT WAS ENOUGH THE BLOOD THAT YOU SHED
IT WAS ENOUGH THAT YOU ROSE FROM THE DEAD
IT WAS ENOUGH TO SET ME FREE
IT WAS ENOUGH THAT YOU DIED FOR ME

(from *It Was Enough* by Larry Bryant)

Murky Waters

Steve was my well-groomed hippie friend in Bible college. Even complying with the school's short-hair code, his hippiness came through. Maybe it was the sandals. Or maybe it was just the laid back way he carried himself. But you could tell — even with short hair — he was a true hippie.

Steve told me that on Shoal Creek there was a great place to swim with a big rope swing. We went looking. When we found the spot, we stood at the base of a BIG tree and looked up. Hanging from a branch high up was a rope; below the rope was brown, murky water. If the fall didn't kill us, something in the water probably would.

Steve climbed the tree to the spot where he could grab the rope. He positioned himself to swing out of the tree and into the water, but he froze. I couldn't believe he chickened out. He said it was too high. Wimp. So I told him to scoot himself down the tree, and I would show him how it's done. He got down. I climbed up. Heights don't bother me too much, so I just kept climbing. I got the rope, held on tightly, looked down...and froze. It seems Steve had a point. It was high. I sheepishly climbed down.

We didn't know it, but a hitchhiker was watching the whole episode from a highway overpass close to where we were. He yelled out to us that he would do it. We watched in amazement as the hitch-hiker climbed the tree, took the rope, swung out over the creek and dropped in the water. Splash. As we looked over the bank to see if he would come up again, he popped his head up out of the water. Steve and I looked at each other as if to say, "Why couldn't we do that?"

Then we did. For the next two hours, Hippie Steve, the hitchhiker and I took turns swinging out over the creek and plunging into the brown water.

For a long time I thought about what happened that day at Shoal Creek. It was one of those times you look back on and think, "That was truly fun." Nothing immoral or illegal. Nobody got hurt (surprisingly). Just a simple, good time.

For me, life often seems murky. It is hard to understand. Decisions are not clear. Things don't often make sense. I see why Paul said that we "see through a glass darkly."

The murkiness is often what makes it hard to move forward. "What's down there?" "What's going to happen?" "What if...?"

Sometimes you have to be lead to swing out over muddy water and let go. I spent my childhood vacations making splashes in crystal clear hotel swimming pools. I can't remember any of the exact moments.

This was different. It was unknown, unpredictable. That's what made it a memory, made it special.

Leaping from the safety of what was familiar and comfortable to me and into something completely uncomfortable and unfamiliar will always cause a reaction. You won't stay the same. I never did. It is much safer, easier and reasonable to stay out of the tree and on the shore. But if you do, you will surely miss out on something new.

The possibility of missing out on an opportunity that God opens up is a risk too big for me to take. I instinctively knew that life is risky no matter how I played it. Risk is built into life. But, for me, nothing would be riskier than playing it safe and then living a life of regret.

I was ready to switch from jumping into murky creeks and leap into real life ministry. It turns out creeks are safer.

Square Peg

Sometimes you can put a square peg in a round hole, you just have to push a lot harder.

Bible college prepared me for everything in ministry: doctrine, organization, Bible interpretation, church structure, ministerial conduct and more. Everything, that is, except relationships.

Knowing it would throw me out of my comfort zone and stretch me to the limit, I decided to leave the safety of my Bible college dorm room to apply for a weekend preaching ministry in a small church. I was nervous. I knew I was going way in over my head, but I had to do it. I was purposely trying to position myself where I could not hide.

When I returned to Ozark in the fall of 1977, I had a car. I was mobile! I was ready to use my ministry skills. I went to the Bible college office and asked if they had leads on churches looking for a weekend preacher. They handed me a list of churches, supposedly within 30 miles.

I called the first one on the list. Steve, the board chairman at Reece Christian Church in Reece, Kansas, answered and invited me to preach that weekend. I accepted and asked him for directions. When he told me how to get there, it seemed like quite a trip. I asked how long it would take. "Oh, the last boy could make it in about 3 hours," he replied. Three hours! Thinking I could do it once and then look for another church, I agreed. After all, it paid $50 a week.

For some reason I kept going back. I made the 3 hour trip each way every weekend during my final two years of college. I never did tell the college office that their "30-minute-drive church list" was deeply flawed.

This uncharted Kansas town was the size of a hubcap. Total

population: 47. I counted! A place where entertainment was not going to a movie or a basketball game. Their entertainment was…special. Using motorcycles, the boys in this town chased down coyotes across open fields. When they got close enough, they popped a wheelie, came down on the coyote and, well, killed it.

In the town of Reece, relationships were everything because… well…there just wasn't anything else. For someone with my introverted nature, Reece was torture.

Shy/city does not mesh with crazy/country. There was no place to hide. Everyone knew I was in town. No place to disappear. No blending in. I felt like I was in a fish bowl.

The firehouse was a dilapidated, garage-type building with a single fire truck. It was actually the most dangerous spot in town. Ready to collapse any minute, kids were warned to stay away. I later learned everyone in town considered themselves firemen. It was the duty of whoever saw the fire first to run to the firehouse, start up the fire truck, drive to the fire and put it out.

Fires happened more times than you would think and provided some of the best entertainment in town. The passing trains often set off sparks that set the wooden bridges on fire. Someone would see the smoke, run to get the fire truck and spray the bridge. They would then refill the fire truck from the pond and back it back into the firehouse. If it weren't for the occasional burning bridge, there would have been little excitement for this city boy.

On my first Sunday at Reece Christian Church, I stood before my new congregation to pray over communion. I looked up at the two elders standing side-by-side staring at me.

On my left was stoned-faced Orville. He was a 6'2", 80 year

old, retired business executive in a crisp tailored suit. Next to him stood Ted, a motorcycle rider. Wild-man Ted faced me with his long hair and shaggy beard wearing a T-shirt with a picture of geese flying over a field. Ted was famous in Reece for his near death motorcycle accident. Legend has it that he wrecked his motorcycle while coasting at 120 mph with his feet on the handle bars and his hands behind his head resulting in the loss of his thumb and forefinger!

Surprisingly, the two men loved and admired each other. They were a living, breathing illustration of what church relationships should be. Vastly different people, united in their faith in Jesus. At the time, I merely saw the visual difference. The significance was lost to me.

The contrasting image of those two opposites on my first official day in ministry is burned into my brain to this day. I didn't know that ministry would put me in contact with such a wide variety of people. I guess I had always assumed that my congregations would be composed of people like the ones I had grown up in church with. That assumption was blown on day 1.

My "by the book" ministry style wasn't fitting with my congregation. I assumed that people everywhere would have the same questions I had, but the people of Reece didn't have any questions at all. They were simple people. They enjoyed their lives and loved their town. It was the last place on earth I would want to put down roots. They didn't want to live anywhere else.

Reece was real. Real people. Real problems. Real struggles. I was prepared for none of it. I wanted to drag them into my world of theology and instead I got sucked into their world of relationships.

Coon Hunting

I knew immediately that I had to try to fit in. I wanted to be a part of Reece. So…I went coon hunting with them. They invited me; I accepted.

On my second weekend in Reece, I found myself running through a thick forest. Pointing my $.99 Walmart flashlight straight ahead of me, my primary objective was to avoid falling into a deep ravine. It was midnight, and I realized if I died out there I wouldn't be discovered until the spring thaw. I had no idea where I was. I was following instructions and hoping I didn't hear banjo music.

I knew nothing about coon hunting, or any kind of hunting for that matter. I envisioned walking in an open field along the edge of a forest taking pot shots at napping raccoons in broad daylight. It turns out I had the wrong picture.

Here's how it all went down. At 7:00 on Saturday night we stopped for pizza. I wondered why since it was starting to get dark. We then spent another hour picking up a coon dog for $1200. Twelve hundred dollars! For what? A dog trained to sniff out raccoons.

Finally…we got to the forest about midnight. "Too late now," I thought. "We can't see a thing."

I'm up for shooting varmints in trees, but I was surprised to find we had to do it in a thick forest, late at night. I had to preach in the morning, and it was way past my bedtime. But God sent me here. I wanted to connect with the people.

Coon hunting is best achieved at night, late at night. Nine Reece locals and me were now on the hunt for a raccoon. Steve handed me a cheap flashlight and a stick and told me if I held the stick in front of my face it would soften the blow of the branches as I ran full steam through the woods. They released the coon dogs and ran after them in a sprint.

My choice was simple. Wait there and die, or run and maybe find my way out of this Kansas forest. I ran. Fast. I fell down in a creek, stumbled up/down hills, and listened for the distant howls of coon dogs. I looked like an escaped convict bolting from Sing Sing.

By the time we caught up with the dogs, they had "treed" the coon. The coon made a run for it. The dogs captured him and killed him. We did nothing but watch. "Why did we even bother to show up?" I thought. We could have released the dogs, gone to bed and waited for the canines to drag home their prey in the morning. We were completely unnecessary. We evidently did it for the adventure of doing something together...I suppose. For a task-driven guy like me, it made no sense.

Welcome to the ministry, Roger.

My Shack

The summer before I got married I lived by myself in a small, vacant shack in Reece—as in run down, holes in the floor, stinky shack. One bedroom, small kitchen, "living" room and a front porch that looked like it might collapse any moment. It's a bit like something the Unabomber would appreciate.

Critters of all varieties called it home. But it was the only available lodging, so I took it. I figured I could endure anything for one summer. I have never lived on a foreign mission field, but this had to be close. I once woke up with a dead mouse in my bed, and another time I saw a snake in the living room as he slithered down a hole in the floor.

The shack was next door to Motorcycle Ted and his wife,

Myra. I knew if I needed help of any kind they would be there for me. They were wonderful people. When I almost burned down the shack trying to cook corn bread in a broiler oven, it was Myra that helped put out the fire. Note: you can't cook corn bread in a broiler oven.

My mom and dad came to visit me in Kansas that summer. Mom gasped when she saw my dumpy house. She thought she raised me better. I guess not.

Over the Cliff

Motorcycle Ted got me a summer job at a construction company in Eldorado, about 30 miles down the highway. My summer routine was grueling: up at 5:00, out the door by 5:30, at the construction office by 6:00 where I was packed/crammed/smashed in with three tobacco chewing workers in the cab of an old, rusty pickup truck. With no seat belts, we drove 45 miles to the construction site each day to pour concrete. I slept. Everyday, unable to move, pressed shoulder to shoulder next to the driver, I snoozed for 45 minutes.

That worked great until one morning when I was awakened by the sound of a foot stomping the floorboard. The driver was smashing the brake trying to stop our pick-up truck. The brakes had failed. I looked out the window just in time to see our truck slide off a fifty-foot cliff, roll over a few times on the way down and land upside down in a creek. No one made a peep. We froze and watched the ground and sky swirl. When the truck stopped, the driver yelled, "Gas leak! Get out before it blows up!" On his advice we climbed out of the back window and scampered up the hill where we all stared down at the truck waiting for it to blow. We had seen too many movies.

I noticed the back of my head felt wet. Realizing I might have a serious injury, I placed my hand on my head and looked at it expecting to see blood. Creek water. I was fine. We were all fine. None of us even went to the hospital except for the driver, and his injury certainly wasn't life threatening. His hand got smashed on the steering wheel from the cab of the truck caving in.

None of us understood how we escaped that day so easily. My fellow truck-mates said it was because "the preacher" was with them. "How silly," I thought.

You may think I would have known how to talk about the Lord with three other men who just gave me credit for their escape from death, but I guess not. I was hired to work construction, and that is all I did. My relationship skills were still not up to the task. Reece didn't solve my inability to relate to people, but it was a good first step.

It was like the first time you release the bicycle your child is on and he crashes into a tree. You say, "Oh, Roger, that was good, really!" Reece was like that for me. I crashed. I never did anything memorable while I was in Reece, but it gave me one big victory. My time there taught me to live with the uncomfortable feeling of relating to people instead of running from it.

This track is a recurring one. My default personality is shyness and I continue to drift toward it unless I continually make a decision to jump it.

Do Something Else

Steve, the chairman of the church board, took me aside one day. He asked me if I had any interests other than ministry. I stumbled around at answering his question, and then he said to me, "Well, Roger, if there is anything else besides ministry you can do, you might want to go do it." He was as kind and compassionate as he could be as he delivered his assessment of my ministerial abilities. I understand why he said it. He did me a big favor by saying it.

Those words were the start of a developing new skill in me: ignoring wise advice from well-meaning people. Given the information he had, Steve was right in saying what he said. But I knew what God put in my heart was bigger than his observation of me.

Jumping the Tradition Track

My Beliefs in Crisis

Sideways Energy

I was secure in my doctrine and could handle myself in a theology debate. I excelled in knowing what I didn't believe and in answering questions nobody cared about.

I was trained to articulate why I didn't believe in miracles, the rapture, gifts of the Spirit, eternal security, women in ministry, salvation by grace, Calvinism and much more. I could also handle any question on hermeneutics, apologetics, New Testament evidences, Pauline epistles, dead sea scrolls, etc. So let's say you came up to me and asked if a Calvinist could be raptured while speaking in tongues; I might actually have an answer for that.

I can't begin to tell you how much it annoyed me that nobody seemed interested in theology. I understood deep theological issues and nobody cared. "What is wrong with these people?" I thought.

Ordinary people struggled with things I couldn't relate to as a kid fresh out of the theological security of Bible College. We were worlds apart. I wanted to answer questions about evolution, end time prophecy and church government. They wanted to know how to get along with their spouse, pay the bills, raise their kids and get over their illnesses.

It was like I was trying to teach a fish to ride a bicycle. The fish didn't want to ride a bike. Ordinary people didn't care about solving complex theological issues. They just wanted to survive the coming week. I realized just how irrelevant my approach to ministry was to real people. It was as if I was trying to get them to pass a test for God.

That was my challenge: introduce people to a God who was real and relevant. Instinctively, I knew that if God were real He would matter in daily life. He should/would make a difference. But I had carefully crafted an approach to ministry that didn't matter. It was irrelevant to everyone except theologians, and they had their minds made up already.

I was searching for a way to make ministry something beyond going through the motions. Something more than church services, weddings, funerals, sermons and lessons. There had to be something more. Something that moved people's lives forward, not just sideways.

Graduated/Married On Same Day

I spent a lot of time in the library at Ozark. Studying was important, but so were the girls. Being shy didn't mean I didn't notice girls. They didn't always notice me, but I noticed them. I even dated a little in high school and college.

In October, 1979, the first semester of my senior year, I was sitting at a table in the library with my brother Jeff (he had enrolled that semester). We were minding our own business when two girls sat at the other end of our table. They were cute! They were reading a book assigned to them in their Christian Womanhood class. Suddenly, a pencil came rolling across the table right at me. I picked it up and preceded to give it back to the girl sitting in the direction the pencil came from. She broke out laughing and declared, "It works." Come to find out, the book she was reading told of ways to get a guy's attention. She tried out the "pencil method" and saw it as a success. I definitely noticed her. She was full of energy and fun. She obviously didn't need a pencil to get a guys attention.

I sought her out over the next few weeks until I had her attention and she agreed to go out with me. In three months time, I knew she was the one. I asked her to marry me during the

Christmas break of 1979. She said, "Yes."

May 10, 1980, turned out to be a busy day. I graduated from Bible college and got married on the same day. After a short/inexpensive honeymoon to Tulsa, my wife, Tammie, and I moved to Eureka, Kansas. Our new home was ten miles from Reece.

I know why they call newlyweds "just married." It means you are just married, nothing else. You are still stupid about marriage, stupid about building a life together, stupid about raising kids, stupid about everything. You're...just married. Nothing else, just married.

A Vacuum

My Bible college training taught me more about what to be against, than what to be for. I knew what I DIDN'T believe more clearly than what I did believe. Back then, and still somewhat this way, the Christian Church denomination was determined not to be confused with Baptists or Charismatics. A part of that equation was to de-emphasize grace and faith while emphasizing discipleship. It left me with the impression that God accepted us on the basis of what we do for him. That approach formed a spiritual vacuum in me.

Shortly, after getting married, I read James Kennedy's *Evangelism Explosion*. It changed my life and ministry perspective forever. It put together the rest of the pieces, completing in me the process Larry's song had started.

Before reading Kennedy's book, I was beginning to understand that Jesus paid for our salvation in full and offers it to us as a free gift. But I still had some reservations. I was trained well in works salvation. I couldn't grasp the idea that our goodness/works had no role to play in our eternal destiny. To me being forgiven by God always required an elusive mixture of God's grace and my good deeds. Kennedy changed that equation for me.

Kennedy's canyon illustration sealed the deal. He explained that salvation is like trying to cross a 100 foot canyon using rope and thread. He said most people approach God like someone tying 50 feet of rope to 50 feet of thread and trying to crawl across the canyon by holding onto the rope/thread combo. Obviously, the thread will break. In his illustration the rope represented the perfect life of Jesus and how He gave to us on the cross. The thread represents our good works, weak and frail.

Then he added that some people try to tie 90 feet of rope (Jesus) to 10 feet of thread (our goodness). The thread still breaks. The result is the same. You hit the canyon floor.

OLD NEW	
TRACK TRACK	
legalism	grace
do	be
weakness	power
cynicism	faith
coping	victory
tradition	scripture
God distant	God inside

Then he nailed me good. Some people tie 99 feet and 11 inches of rope to one inch of thread. But the thread still breaks. The only solution is to use 100 feet of rope by trusting Jesus for 100 percent of our salvation. And that's the one thing I never did…until then.

No longer was I trying to earn my way to Heaven by working hard for God. I did something that before would have been unimaginable: I trusted what Jesus did for me on the cross without reservation. I finally and fully realized that I had…a Savior.

All of my church attendance and all of my Bible college had led me to trust myself for my salvation and relationship with

God. I knew the facts about Jesus. But I somehow became convinced that what He did for me on the cross was not enough. I believed I had to complete the price He paid. I had to finish it.

Due to that simple clarification, the good news of the Gospel made complete sense to me for the first time. Larry's song had altered my perspective, but Kennedy's book pushed me the rest of the way to a 100% change.

The Cable Guy

My position at the church was part time, so immediately after the honeymoon I began job hunting in Eureka. The only job available in the town was working for the cable TV company. Cable was important to small, rural towns that existed in the middle of nowhere. For them, it was cable or nothing. They couldn't even pick up the networks without cable in that region of Kansas. Thirteen channels. CNN just launched and soon after followed ESPN. I got the job. I was the official cable installer for our town. You wanted cable; you got me.

Three months after I took this job, lightning struck our cable tower. Cable towers in Kansas were tall because there were no hills to put them on. Everything was flat, so the tower had to be extra tall. Ours was just short of 600 feet straight up. Two football field lengths, straight up in the air. With a triangular diameter of two feet and held down by guide wires, it had a tendency to sway in the Kansas wind. The lightning blew out a bulb which didn't seem like a big deal to me, but the manager took it very seriously. He didn't like the thought of some wayward airplane clipping our tower in half because the pilot couldn't see it. Using a heavy leather safety belt, I climbed the two foot wide tower the distance of two football fields and replaced the bulb. It took me over an hour to climb to the top. If my arms got tired, I could hook the belt to the tower and lean back. That way my arms could dangle down and rest.

The height really didn't bother me. I rationalized that if I were only 3 feet off the ground I could certainly hold on to the metal structure. No question. So what's the difference if I'm hundreds of feet up? To me it was all perspective.

Besides, they paid me triple time! I was happy to risk life and limb for an extra fourteen dollars an hour. Big money to me then. I changed the bulb and safely arrived back on earth feet first.

When lightning again zapped our top beacon a few months later, I knew I was in for another climb. Having now made the vertical trip once, I felt confident enough to leave the heavy, leather, safety belt on the ground. Wearing cut off jeans and a T-shirt, I took my wrench and bulb up 600 feet while the manager watched from the ground with binoculars. I reached the top, wrapped my legs through the metal tower bars and tried to release the glass globe that covered the bulb. The thick glass globe weighed about forty pounds and was the size of a large lamp shade. It was stuck.

After several attempts I changed position to get a better grip. That didn't work. The only option left was to sit directly on top of the tower and wrap my legs around the globe while I tried to unlatch it. The Kansas wind was blowing. The tower was swaying. And I was sitting on top of a skinny tower 600 feet in the air…with no safety gear. The 360 degree view was amazing. I looked over to see a helicopter flying by BELOW me. That's when I realized how really high up I was. I removed the globe, changed the bulb and climbed down.

On top of that tower I could see for miles. It was exhilarating. The distance from the ground and noise from the wind made it impossible to communicate with anyone. It was just me, the Kansas wind and open sky in all directions.

That's how I looked at life, full of space and possibility in every direction: dangerous but exhilarating. And worth pushing the limits.

Going Home

One Sunday Wally showed up at our church in Reece. I'm not sure how he found it all the way from Morehead, Kentucky, but there he was. He had been sent by a small group of people looking for a minister. Wayne Smith, my home church minister, had recommended me.

Wally wanted me to come back to Kentucky to take over a small fledgling church in a university town nestled on the fringe of the Appalachian Mountains. It would be my first full time ministry, and going back to Kentucky sounded great.

In the dead of winter, Tammie and I packed our earthly possessions in a Ryder truck (a scene that would later be repeated two more times, ironically with less stuff each time), and with car in tow, plowed through the snow. I was coming back to Kentucky.

I took over the small church in Morehead that was trying to recover from strife and legalism. The former chairman of the board and former senior minister hated each other. Only weeks before I arrived, the chairman started the practice of walking out of the services and sitting in his car when the minister began to preach. Finally, the board fired the preacher. Then most of the board resigned and left the church. The remnant hired me.

I was a young preacher trying to figure out what it meant to be a minister. After years of living and studying in the religion of the denomination I grew up in, I knew there had to be more. This couldn't possibly be all there was to God, ministry, life and church. Surely not. But what?

Social Justice and the Big Satellite Dish

What should ministry look like? I agonized/toiled over that question. I wanted to do it right. Ministry should make a difference, I reasoned. That's what I wanted more than anything: to make a difference. Somehow. Somewhere. I didn't want to go through the motions. I didn't want to play church like I had while growing up. I wanted something more. Shouldn't God's people make an impact in the community? But how?

I remembered hearing Tony Campolo speak at Bible College during my first semester. It had an impact on me. I read books by social justice advocates like Ron Sider, John Howard Yoder and Jim Wallis. Their message made sense at the time: help the poor. The Bible talks a lot about the poor, so I decided to make a difference by helping them. After all, I was in eastern Kentucky, the edge of the Appalachian Mountains.

> **I'm not called to change the world but to serve the ONE who did.**
> --Craig Jutila

I shared my thoughts about poverty with the local pastors at the Rowan County Ministerial Association (a lively bunch for sure). They laughed at me. That angered me. How can these old curmudgeons (who turned out to be smarter than me) be so apathetic? So nonchalant? I was determined not to let that happen to me.

I figured if I could help the poor, then they would understand God loved them. Then they would put their faith in Jesus and get involved in our church. That became the focus of my ministry.

But it never worked.

We started a food bank. People heard about it and called the church. We took them food. Simple.

One time in particular, a woman called the church saying she needed food. I took food to her house. As I pulled into her driveway, I couldn't help but notice a satellite dish about the size of Vermont in the yard. This was back when few homes had satellite dishes. I knocked on the door. Someone yelled, "Come in!" I entered the home to see about six people in a darkened family room watching a huge TV screen. I told them I was from the church and was here to deliver some food. A lady on the couch pointed to the kitchen table and shouted, "Just put it on the table!" I did and then left. No one got up to help. No one thanked us. They obviously felt entitled to receive our help. And this same type of scenario repeated itself.

If you read history you will find that the Christians who did most for the present world were precisely those who thought most of the next. It is since Christians have largely ceased to think of the other world that they have become so ineffective in this. --C.S. Lewis

I changed the policy after that. From then on I required people to come to the church and fill out a one page form to receive food. Most refused. They said they could get free food other places without having to fill out a form. Wow. Evidently I was asking too much of them.

It took me about three years of this to figure out just how…difficult…complicated…frustrating "social justice" would be.

My view of the church's mission shifted. It was becoming more difficult for me to believe that God wanted us to invest significant time and money in helping people that didn't seem interested in helping themselves. They obviously didn't want us talking to them about the Lord. What most wanted was a quick, easy hand out. Somehow the love of Jesus didn't flow out of the grocery bags.

A few people in need started attending the church without asking for anything. Those are the people we began to help. We helped them financially and taught them how to take responsibility for themselves. Most of them saw God do positive things for them economically. Peggie, a new church attendee, heard what God's Word said about her and began to realize she had more value than she thought. She got a good job, got off food stamps, stabilized financially and even started giving. Others were experiencing the same thing. I was beginning to get it. A job is the best social justice program.

I began to realize God did not call me to solve all of society's problems. That's a burden nobody is called to carry. At Kidz Blitz, the ministry I later founded, we talk to pastors everyday. One pastor from Tennessee was discouraged and beaten down by the weight of ministry. When we told him that he was not responsible to feed, clothe and provide housing for all the needy people in his area, the pastor almost went into shock. He never considered that possibility. His attitude toward the ministry changed immediately as he felt this burden lift. Many times our drive to "change the world" ends up frustrating us. Little by little we start to carry burdens God never intended for us.

Personally, I find it ironic that the Jesus of the Gospels did so little for the poor. That statement shocks most people. Think about it. The Bible does, however, say often that Jesus preached to the poor. His words helped them more than a handout.

Jesus never started a soup kitchen, a food pantry, a clothing bank or a housing project. With the exception of feeding lunch to the 5000 who came to hear Him speak, He never did ANY-

THING personally for the poor. If He did, the Gospel writers didn't record it.

When I point that out to people, they tell me Jesus was too poor to help others. I'm not so sure. He had a treasurer (Judas). Thanks to the wise men, He hit the gold, frankincense and myrrh lottery when He was two years old. And when He was crucified, the soldiers didn't want to cut up his expensive robe, so they threw dice for it. When Judas wanted to sell some expensive perfume to give the money to the poor, Jesus wouldn't let him.

When we help people, we should do it out of love, not because economic empowerment is the focus of the church. The mandate is to make disciples, not level the world economically. Our mission is eternal, not socioeconomic.

Even the church in Acts limited its financial resources to helping people within the church. They never made it a priority to solve the economic woes of Judea or Palestine.

The Good Samaritan helped a man in need that crossed his path. I like that approach. He didn't start a "Left for Dead Ministry Center" in Jericho. Broad sweeping programs are not as effective as individual expressions of compassion. Our church began to help people God brought to us, rather than start a broad-based program trying to raise the poverty level in Morehead.

This epiphany began the process of remolding my ministry focus. What should be MY mission? What am I called to do? If it is not to sociologically/economically change the world, what is it? What? I was willing to do anything for my ministry to be effective, relevant and powerful. But I wasn't willing to reduce Jesus to a middle-eastern social worker and our church into something akin to a government agency. That was not going to happen.

Captain Hook

Once I went to see June Hook, a woman who visited our church. She had a house on Cave Run Lake. That was odd. Since the lake was in the Daniel Boone National Forest, virtually no one had homes on the lake. But she did. They called her "Captain Hook." She had a modest home in front of a mountain. When I pulled into her driveway, I noticed her front yard packed with boats and campers. She met me at the door and invited me in. I asked about the boats and campers in the front yard. She told me they paid her $30 a month to park there. Wow, I was impressed. I told her she had quite the business going because she had about 25-30 parked there. She laughed. "I have over 300!" said Captain Hook. She took me out back and showed me how she had carved off the side of the mountain and used it for boat/camper rental space. You would never know it to look at her, but she was one savvy business lady. Captain Hook became a good friend and active part of the church.

She told me how she was sick for years and took massive amounts of medicine daily. She began to read/study God's word and came to the conclusion that God didn't want her to live that way. Her health improved dramatically and rapidly. No more pills. She was healthy and vibrant.

I couldn't help but think: how many more people are there who took God at His word and experienced dramatic results? How many stories exist that we have never heard about? How many Captain Hook's are out there?

Through Captain Hook's influence, the Morehead Yacht Club asked me to become their honorary chaplain. I accepted and prayed over the fleet at the annual spring ceremony, asking God to bless and protect the boaters. Though I never owned a boat, I enjoyed telling people I was the chaplain of the Morehead Yacht Club. Later I learned that the club annually gets a preacher to pray over the boats because so many boat captains sail while drunk. They want all the protection they can get.

I have still never been on a real yacht, but I can claim I was once chaplain of a yacht club. That ought to come in handy someday. But as cool as it was for the moment, being chaplain of the Morehead Yacht Club was not a destiny that harnessed my passion. I didn't want to be remembered for it. Here lies Roger T. Fields, nobody sank while he was chaplain of the Morehead Yacht Club.

Mica's Miracle

Less than a year after moving to Morehead, Tammie got pregnant and gave birth to our first child, Terra. Eighteen months later she gave birth to Mica. The girls were amazing. Becoming a dad changed me forever.

Then a crisis hit, one that rocked my world and theology forever.

Mica, now 18 months old, became very sick. Her hair wasn't growing. She was pale. She passed chunks of undigested food multiple times everyday. She hadn't gained any weight since she was six months old. The doctor was not optimistic and told us she was "failing to thrive." In Mica's particular case, that was another way of saying that she was dying. We were without health insurance, afraid and desperate.

Bible college classes became distant memories. Theological arguments were irrelevant. Denominational lines grew faint. It was no longer important to feel superior to other people/

churches/denominations.

I needed a miracle…fast.

I had preached that God no longer healed anyone. I believed healing happened during Bible days but not today. I was taught that since we now have the Bible, we don't need miracles or healing. That made sense to me. Besides, it was convenient for me to believe that God didn't heal when I didn't have anything that needed healing anyway.

It was easy for me to let my own experience interpret, and thus limit, the Bible. I realized how selfish my God-doesn't-do-miracles-today theology was. I only taught about a God who did what I needed from Him at the time. And up until then, I hadn't needed anything or anybody healed.

But now it was different. It was MY girl who was dying. So I was willing to try anything, including dumping my God-limiting theology.

We asked some of the church leaders to come and pray over Mica. Having grown up in a church that seldom prayed for healing and after graduating from a college that taught me God stopped doing that years ago, I was in unfamiliar territory. My theology did not allow for what I was about to do. I was amazed how easily I discarded my doctrine when faced with a life and death challenge.

In the living room of our small, brick home, we placed our hands on Mica's head and made it very clear to God what we wanted. A few minutes later we stopped praying and looked at Mica. Color came into her face. Everyone was amazed. I brushed it off attributing it to our hands warming her head and increasing blood flow.

The next day she stopped passing undigested food. Within a week she gained a pound, no small feat when she didn't weigh hardly anything to begin with. The doctor checked her and said, "It is as if someone waved a magic wand over this child." I was so surprised by the doctors comment that I didn't know what to say. Tammie and I left the office in amazement.

She continued to gain weight. The doctor continued to verify her advancing health. She had completely overcome the illness. As I write this today, she is 26, healthy and the ball-of-fire leader of the TEA Party movement in Kentucky.

Mica's instant recovery changed my theology and life forever. That day God got bigger.

Without realizing it then, I had been making the classic mistake of letting my experience shape the Bible instead of allowing the Bible to shape my experience. The Bible never changed to match my experience; but my experience COULD change to match the Bible. That became my objective: to see my family reflect all that God promised in His Word.

Mica's healing was a total game changer for me. Because of it I thought more and more about how I had allowed my unbelief to almost rob me of my daughter. As Mica continued to thrive with no symptoms of any ailments, I pondered these things in my heart.

What would have happened if we had not taken action? What if we hadn't prayed boldly? What if we had given up? What if we had accepted her illness as being God's will? What if we had hidden behind easy religious slogans? "It must be God's will." "Well...now you know, God is sovereign." Huh? What would have happened?

From that day on I decided to err on the side of faith. If I was going to make a mistake, I was going to do it by having too much faith. Even if I got disappointed, I figured I could stand before God and say, "Well, I just believed this stuff too much I guess." I couldn't see how God could be upset with that. But I didn't want to stand before God one day and say, "Well, I just didn't believe what You said in the Bible. Oops."

It Was the Best of Times...

All of my life I had been on one theological track. It was all I knew. Then within a couple of years our church changed... dramatically. It transitioned from a legalistic, contentious church into a loving, grace-filled church. We actually saw God do stuff. We were on a new track.

Praise and worship became vibrant. We prayed for any and every situation. Church was fun. Instead of rushing home after church, people stayed around. They shared together, prayed together. It was exhilarating. I had never seen anything like it.

But it was a bitter/sweet time with a tumultuous down side.

There were those who had long since left the church who liked the old track better. They criticized me from afar. That bothered me deeply. I didn't want to disappoint anyone, particularly those who cared about our church.

Wayne Smith, the pastor I grew up under was upset. It was through his recommendation that the church hired me from Kansas. Later after we built a new church building, he dropped in to see it. He noticed our kitchen was unfinished due to budget constraints. A week later two men showed up at the church and began to measure the kitchen. Two weeks after that they showed up again and installed new cabinets and finished the kitchen. Wayne paid for it. He was good to me.

But when the church changed its name and its direction, and

was veering away from our denominational ways, Wayne was flat out mad. He went to my parents and told them how angry he was about what I was doing in Morehead. I hated it that my parents were dragged into my controversial decisions concerning the church.

I had a lot of sleepless nights. But I knew down deep what I was doing was right. The impact on the lives of the people convinced me that this was what God was leading me to do.

It was difficult to turn my back on the only denomination I ever knew, the independent Christian Church. I don't mean to indict the entire denomination. Today, it is much more grace-oriented. Then it was a legalistic denomination that ridiculed anything supernatural. Although they always denied being a denomination, most every Christian Church believed the same theology and conducted church in the same way. It was my theological home, my life. But I had had enough of that track.

I could never go back. For me, the church in Morehead had transformed into what church was meant to be. I liked the new track. It was fresh, relevant and exciting. Theologically and experientially, I had traded up.

I had no intention of making any more changes in my life. I had a great family. My theology was settled. Morehead was my home. I was content. Life was good. Change was stressful, and I had already experienced enough of it. More than anything else I wanted a calm life without change, without stress and without conflict. I was on a pleasant track and wanted to stay there.

Jumping the Settled Track

Moving Away from the Home We Planned

Stayed Long Enough On This Mountain

I was comfortable in Morehead. The town was small (8000), but Morehead State University livened it up. The college students made it a fun place to live. The church was doing well, and I loved the ministry there. Cave Run Lake was only 10 miles down the road, a large lake for boating, skiing, fishing and swimming. Morehead is a wonderful place to live, raise a family and play.

Tammie and I were settling in for life. We bought twelve acres just outside of town. The property was a large, wooded area elevated above the rest of the subdivision. We called it our "mountain." We moved into a large, mobile home on the property where we lived with the intention of building a house there.

It was picturesque, even tranquil. Most of the time.

There was the time I was burning brush on the front acre and let the fire get away from me. It's amazing what a big wind can do with a little fire and a bunch of dry brush. The Morehead Fire Department came out with several trucks and put out the fire. The fire chief scolded me and threatened to charge me if it happened again. He was still sore about the time my trash fire rekindled on its own while I was at church and his department had to come out on Sunday morning. I was getting too familiar with the fire department, so I never burned anything on the property again. They now knew me by name. But our "mountain" was looking better all of the time. We anticipated the day we could start construction on our house. Morehead was our home, where we planned to settle.

Then something began to happen inside of me. I became restless. I was beginning to realize God had other plans for us. Morehead was not our final destination. But what was?

When I began to sense that our time there was coming to an end, it saddened me. God had done so much in our lives in Morehead. As I continued to pastor the church, I wondered. Where was God leading us?

I like to work outside. The departure from the demands of ministry and office work renews me. After days of study/preaching/funerals/weddings/counseling I need to do something physical, something that gets my body moving. Much to the dismay of our elder board, I often chose to mow the church lawn. I loved the sunshine, the physical exercise and the feeling that I was conquering something. In ministry, you don't often get that feeling.

OLD TRACK	NEW TRACK
settled down	moving on
roots	wings
secure	risk
familiar	unfamiliar
safe	scary
friends/family	strangers
stay forever	go now

One day was different from all the rest.

I was mowing the grass when for the first—and only—time in my life, I heard God speak to me audibly. Three words. "Go to Tampa." I whipped around to see who crept up on me. No one was there. I stopped, looked around and continued to mow. "What the heck was that?" I thought as I mowed.

I told Tammie what happened. She knew also that God was moving us somewhere else. Maybe Tampa was the place. But I was not ready to leave Morehead, the place I loved, the church where I invested so much of my life.

Several months later I was in line at an office supply store waiting to check out. It was snowing outside. As the line proceeded ahead toward the clerk, an over-whelming sensation came over me to tell the clerk I was moving to Florida. I distinctly remember telling God, "No way am I going to tell this clerk that I am going to Florida. He will think I am crazy and since he doesn't know me he couldn't care less if I moved to Florida. I'm not doing it." I'm not sure about the spiritual ramifications of refusing to obey God, but it can't be good. Nevertheless, there was no way my shyness would allow me to do something like that. Then what happened truly stunned me.

I was next in line. Having settled the issue by refusing to mention Florida to the clerk, I was at ease as I laid my office supplies in front of him on the counter. He looked straight at me and said these words, "I think I want to go to Florida. Do you want to go to Florida?" I was speechless. I mumbled something. Can't remember what it was, but something. I paid him and walked out into the snow, got in my car and drove back to the church. I knew then something was up.

A couple of days later, as I was mulling over what happened in the store, I opened my Bible. I have always taught that it is bad theology to open your Bible randomly and read what is on the page in the belief that God directed you to that spot. God does not work that way. How childish to think you can open your Bible, read a verse and think that God led you to open your Bible to that spot at that moment.

I opened my Bible to the first chapter of the Book of Deuteronomy. Verse 6 jumped off the page at me.

You have dwelt long enough at this mountain.
(Deuteronomy 1:6 NKJV)

I knew what I had to do.

A few months later I found myself bumping along southbound on interstate 75 with my arm hanging out the window of a Ryder truck. I was headed to Florida with my family, our clothes, a water bed, a couple random pieces of furniture and the girls' toys. To earn extra cash for our new start we sold most of our stuff in a yard sale. We were moving to Tampa to start a church. I was uprooting my wife, Tammie, and our two girls, Terra and Mica. Tammie was enthusiastic about the move, and our two young girls thought we would be at the beach every day. It was a great adventure to them. But deep down I wondered if I had lost my mind.

Welcome to the Sunshine State

We pulled into Summit West Apartments after dark, left the truck there and headed to a hotel for the night. The next morning, we came back to unload the truck. The reality of being in a new city with no friends to help us unload hit Tammie hard. She broke down crying while we moved our things inside. It hit her that we were now alone in a big city without family and without friends. The move was more emotionally draining than we expected.

There's a lot about Florida they don't put in the travel brochures: fire ants, bugs, crime galore, bugs, sticky air, mosquitoes big enough to open screen doors, and more bugs.

We moved to Tampa in August of 1989, but the move was quickly appearing to be a ministry set back of epic proportions. I was beginning to wonder how I missed God's leading. His voice seemed clear enough at the time, but things were not working out. I thought following the will of God meant smooth sailing, no problems and money left over.

Before starting the new church, I got a job selling pagers for a company called Metagram. Pagers were hot back when cell service was through-the-roof expensive. Selling was hard work. But somehow, out of several thousand salesmen, I was number 3 in the Southeast United States, and yet I was struggling to pay the bills.

Then we met the Florida fire ants. Tammie was talking to some new friends outside of our apartment door. She didn't realize she was standing in a large fire ant hill. We hadn't learned yet that our barefoot Kentucky ways do not work in Florida. The ants climbed up her bare leg past her knee and began stinging her. Ant stings covered her swollen leg and foot, and she was in intense pain for several days. In hindsight, we should have gone to the emergency room, but we couldn't afford it.

Christmas came. That Christmas was, for me, the worst ever. Tampa temperatures dipped into the 30's. Tampa Electric Co. could not supply enough electricity for people to heat their homes. So they resorted to roaming blackouts. That means they turned off the electricity to sections of town for several hours at a time so they could power the other sections. Christmas Eve found us with no electricity, sitting in the dark with food uncooked in the oven. Now, not only were we broke, we had no electricity and we were cold. Visions of sugar plums were not dancing in my head.

Amazingly, today my family does not remember that as a horrible Christmas. The girls thought it was great. We sat together in a candlelit family room. They loved it. I felt like I had failed my family. But they took it as an adventure, the way I should have seen it. It still amazes me that families can go through the same experience and interpret it differently. I had obviously failed to remember the real reason for Christmas.

Tammie was always resourceful and made sure the girls had a good Christmas. She made low-cost gifts from stuff we already had and managed to fix a great meal from a limited budget. We plodded along trying to put down roots in our new community, hoping to make Tampa home and recapture what we felt in Morehead.

We had rarely locked our doors in Morehead. We drank tap water there. Shoes were optional. Strangers were friends. During the first year in Tampa, 4 of our bikes were stolen, we weren't even sure we should shower in the water much less drink it, and we were learning remedial Spanish. We became default fans of the losingest team in sports history, the Tampa Bay Buccaneers.

A few months after Christmas, I started our new church and immediately discovered that Tampa, Florida culture was not the same as Morehead, Kentucky culture. We were experiencing culture shock which made starting the church a struggle. Not in the Bible belt anymore, church in Tampa was not a dominant part of Florida culture. We always had less than 100 people attend church on Sunday mornings, and we were never able to gain any traction. I wasn't ready to pastor in Florida or start a new church from scratch. The success we had in Kentucky did not transfer to Florida.

Like most failures, something positive emerged.

The best thing that happened with that church was meeting Ken Dovey. When I met Ken, he had a rocking youth group… with no church base. The kids came from different churches and met together on Tuesday nights. He taught them to share their faith, walk with God and accept new kids that came to the group. He was raising up leaders that still serve God today. I was impressed. So later when I needed someone to help me with my new ministry, Kidz Blitz, I called Ken.

But I was learning a lot about people, life and ministry. I knew, someday, somewhere, that would pay off.

Don't Drink the Water

Finances were beginning to look a little better, so we moved to a larger apartment made of orange stucco. One Saturday the girls, Terra, who was seven, and Mica, who was five, and I were at the pool while Tammie was out. The girls told me they were thirsty. This posed a dilemma. Should I gather up all of towels and stuff to walk us back to the apartment for water? That seemed to be too much trouble. I gave the girls strict orders to stay out of the pool and on the towels while I ran back to the apartment for water.

I dashed a short distance to the other side of the building and up the stairs into the apartment. I grabbed a large Texaco mug from the cabinet and filled it with drinking water from a white jug under the sink. I ran the mug back to the pool where Terra and Mica were patiently waiting. I gave them the mug. Both took a sip, turned up their nose and told me the water didn't taste good. I was a bit put out that they didn't like the water I had just worked so hard to bring back for them.

To demonstrate that the water was fine I took several big gulps and handed it back. They wanted nothing to do with it. So I drank some more to make my point. It didn't work. They would not drink the water.

One of my less-than-flattering characteristics is that I do not like to admit I am wrong. So when I noticed the water tasted a little funny, I wasn't about to admit it. "It's this water or nothing," I told them.

Shortly after, we left the pool and returned to the apartment. Tammie came home and the girls told her how I brought water to the pool that didn't taste good. "Where did you get the water?" she asked me. I told her I got it from our jug of drinking water under the sink. She opened the cabinet, held up the jug and said, "This one?" "That's the one," I replied. She gave me a mortified look, placed her hand over her mouth and said, "That's fertilizer!"

Apparently, I drank nearly a quart of Super Bloom.

Reverse This

In 1984 after our second child was born, Tammie and I thought God was done with growing our family. We helped Him out by getting a vasectomy. Seven years later we started questioning that decision. Did we act too quickly? Did we act on our own plan? What was God's plan for our family? We prayed. We asked God to show us His will with our family. It was a simple prayer. One of those - throw it out there, forget about it and see what happens later - prayers. God surprised us by jumping quickly on this one. I think maybe He was like, "It's about time you got with My plan." A week after we prayed, we got a call from my brother Jeff. Jeff knew NOTHING about our thoughts concerning our family or our prayer to get into God's will where our children are concerned. Jeff said, "Teresa (his wife) and I heard from God that we are supposed to offer you $2500 to use for a vasectomy reversal."

"What? Are you serious? What do you know?" We felt like somehow they had invaded our thoughts. They had, through the all-knowing mind of Christ!

We knew what the next step was. We found a place where the success rate of vasectomy reversals was 95%. We had to travel to New Braunfels, TX. It is amazing what $2500, a bunch of caring friends (who took care of our 2 children and gave us money for food and hotel expenses) and a God who wants us to have more children can do!

We went to Texas in May of 1991. I had surgery. Tammie got

pregnant in October. Shannon, our 3rd daughter, was born August 4, 1992. Morgan, our 4th daughter, was born in 1994. Our family was now complete.

Our Brush with AIDS

I was now the father of four girls.

A few years later, we were sitting in a friend's house visiting with them before Christmas. In the course of the conversation, we shared that a friend of ours in the church had died of AIDS. Mary (not her real name) had contracted the disease from her first husband who later left her for another man. As I told the story, a scary realization came over Tammie. Mary, who gave birth to her own child at the same time Shannon was born, worked in our church nursery. Tammie recalled that one Sunday, when we picked up Shannon after the service, Mary let us know that she had breast fed Shannon. She and Tammie had a standing agreement: if the other one's baby got hungry in church, each could nurse the other's child. Suddenly, it hit Tammie. Mary, while infected with AIDS, had nursed Shannon.

As soon as we were in the car, Tammie reminded me of what Mary had done. When she first heard about Mary having AIDS, Tammie had forgotten about her nursing Shannon a year earlier. We had both forgotten. We were now terrified at the thought of our girl having HIV. Knowing that it might take years for the disease to mature, we knew we had to get her tested immediately.

We prayed over Shannon much the way we prayed over Mica years earlier. No wishy-washy, mamby-pamby prayer. We laid our hands on her and told the disease where to go.

I then took her to the clinic where they took a blood sample.

They told us they would do one test and would only do a second test if the first one tested positive. Because of the approaching holidays, it would take several days to get the results. We waited over Christmas to find out whether or not Shannon was HIV positive. Another troubling Christmas.

The clinic called me after the holidays and told me to come in. They wanted me to sign a release for a second test. I was devastated.

Ron, the senior pastor of the church where I was serving by that time, drove me to the clinic. I went to the nurse on duty. She checked the records. There was a mistake. The first test was negative. There was no need for a second test. Shannon was fine. I slid down the wall almost collapsing in relief. We dodged a bullet.

God was faithful to us…again.

Don't Mess with Tammie

A big reason why I was able to jump tracks was because of Tammie. She is a tough girl, able to deal with just about anything.

East Lake Mall was once a thriving shopping area but was beginning to deteriorate. It had slipped into a deserted array of dying stores. We still went there at times because it was close to our church, but it was becoming a hangout for teen gangs. Fewer and fewer people shopped there.

One day Tammie took our girls, plus two other young girls, to the mall. As she lead her tribe of 6 girls, ages 6 months to 12 years old, through an area void of the normal hustle and bustle of most malls, she saw a young man approaching her. She could tell he was headed straight toward her with a purpose. He was wearing a hooded sweat shirt with his hands in his pockets.

He walked within inches pointing something, that looked like a gun, at her from inside his jacket pocket. He demanded her purse. Tammie exclaimed, "No, I'm not giving you my purse!" and quickly walked away. I guess that never happened to him before because he didn't seem to know what to do. He just walked away. She changed course, marched straight to the security office and reported him. A security officer swiftly apprehended him and placed him under arrest.

Tammie is tough. That's one reason we were able to make it through all the challenges of starting a new ministry from scratch. Most women would have cracked under the threat of harm. That thug messed with the wrong girl.

My New Gig

Shortly before Shannon's brush with AIDS, I "merged" our struggling church with another, larger church. Actually, it was more like a takeover than a merger. We were absorbed into the larger church. I went to work as an associate pastor at Living Water Church. Some of the people from our church went with us.

This was my first time on staff at a church without being the lead pastor. I loved it. I missed preaching, but I loved being under less stress. No financial pressure. No stress over discontented people. No feeling rejected when attendance was low.

I had a great gig: weddings, funerals, counseling, organizing the ushers, etc. And I got to sit in one of the big chairs on the platform during Sunday services. It was a walk in the park.

I was content — slightly bored — but content. For the first time in years, our family was stable. That was a good feeling.

Forgotten Letter

I always found it cool when God would do something surprising just to show He was guiding me. It's like driving along a highway unsure of where you are going and suddenly seeing a sign to your destination city. I never demanded or even expected God to do that, but I appreciated when He did. It was an extra bonus.

When our church moved to a new location, I got a cool office overlooking beautiful East Lake. Looking for something to decorate my new space, I started going through stuff I had stored away. I came across a letter that took my breath away. My grandfather, Finnell L. Fields, wrote me a letter when I was two days old, dated October 23, 19-a-long-time-ago. Regrettably, I have no memory of him. He died from a heart attack when I was four. Rummaging through boxes, 35 years later, I found his letter in an old envelope stored away in a box.

It is now framed on my office wall. It contained a prayer for me. Here is part of what it said:

> *My prayer to you will be divine guidance to aid you to become a servant of mankind both intellectually and spiritually. I pray your life will be happy and full of loving kindness.*

My dad's dad was a State Representative in Kentucky, a high school principal and a godly man. He helped shape our family. I will always be grateful for that.

When I so often felt like I was floundering in life, surprises like this one reassured me that God was with me, guiding me…even from my first days.

Father's Day gift 2009

(Left) Mica
(Top) Terra
(Right) Shannon
(Bottom) Morgan

Jim Wideman's Genius Bar
CMX 20011

(Left to Right)
Karen Rhodes
Spencer Click
Roger
Jim Wideman
Jenny Funderburke
Jen Galley
Photo courtesy of
Carla Geary Photography

(above) Roger's "shack" in Reece, Kansas

Roger's brother, Jeff
Jeff's wife, Teresa
Tammie
Roger
2008

The picture from the
Rock Church KBL
event that made the
event worth it
1996

Terra in front of the Capitol on a Kidz Blitz Tour 1998

Terra's kids Rainey (6), Quay (8)

Children's ministry friends: Dale Hudson, Roger and Ryan Frank

early Kidz Blitz Live event

Ken Dovey teachng at CMX 2011

Mica leading a TEA Party rally
Photo courtesy of Gene Linzy Photography

Children's Ministry Expo 2011
Terra Harrison, Teresa Fields, Amanda Crowell,
Ande Long, Tanya Tarp, Alexis Jones

Shannon riding a steer in Maryland
for her 16th birthday

Roger with Jim Wideman
at a memorial for children's
ministry leader Harold Davis

Tammie and the girls in 1994

Tammie and Forrest

Roger on Cave Run Lake the summer before leaving Morehead

Director Chris Williams smashing grits at Kidz Blitz Live

Director Donnie Slade at Kidz Blitz Live

Michael Chanley on a Kidz Blitz Live tour

Director Greg Baird

Ken Dovey "poofing" a volunteer at Kidz Blitz Live

Roger and Tammie at a Halloween party with daughter Mica and her husband John

Roger's parents Tom and Clara Fields on a trip to Alaska

Morgan, age 17, and Roger

(above) Roger and Tammie at Living Water Church
in Tampa 1993

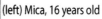

(left) Mica, 16 years old

(left) Terra and her husband Duane on their 10 year
anniversary

(below) Terra and Tammie with
Terra's kids Rainey (L) and Quay (R)

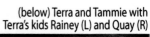

MTV NETWORKS
A VIACOM COMPANY

Robin E. Silverman
Senior Vice President and Deputy General Counsel
Intellectual Property and Litigation

September 12, 2001

Mr. Roger Fields, President
Character Creations
301 United Court, Suite 4
Lexington, KY 40509

Re: Kidz Blitz Live

Dear Mr. Fields:

I am writing on behalf of MTV Networks, a division of Viacom International Inc., which owns and operates the Nickelodeon programming service. A flyer advertising "Kidz Blitz Live" was recently brought to my attention, in which the event is described as being "Nickelodeon-Style". It is our understanding that this event has no connection with Nickelodeon and we are concerned that your use is likely cause confusion as to a possible affiliation between your event and Nickelodeon. We therefore request that no future uses of the Nickelodeon name (or any other MTV Networks' trademark) be made without MTVN's written consent.

We appreciate your anticipated cooperation in this matter. This letter is written without prejudice to any of our rights or remedies, all of which are expressly reserved.

Sincerely,

Robin E. Silverman

The letter received from MTV Networks on 9-12-01

a friend's son and Morgan in original Kidz
Blitz Live T-shirts

(right) Roger preaching in Tampa

2009 (L to R) Duane, Rainey, Terra, Quay, Tammie, Roger, Shannon, Nevaeh, Mica, John, Morgan

2006 Kidz Blitz staff trip to Disney World (couples L to R) Robin and Brian Blair,
Donnie and Christy Slade, Roger and Tammie, Chris and Kate Williams,
Ken and Melissa Dovey, Kevin and Michelle Kern.

Roger in front of his first church in Reece, Kansas.
Yep, that's the way we abbreviate service in rural Kansas.

Roger, age 6

Roger, 7th grade

Roger and Tammie's wedding day

(below) Roger in highschool

(below) Roger in Bible college

Shannon in an original Kidz Blitz
Live T-shirt on a VA Beach KBL tour

(below) Church Roger pastored in Morehead, Kentucky

(below) 2006 Roger and granddaughter, Rainey, on Blitz Farm where Roger currently lives

Roger and Tammie
2007

Jumping the Honor Track

Releasing The Honor

I Got Tricked

In a way, I was tricked into being a children's pastor. Come to find out later, that's how most people get into children's ministry.

Jane Hillman, our other associate pastor and children's pastor, left. She began a traveling ministry to help churches with legal and organizational challenges. Her brother, Larry, took over the children's ministry. Both were good ministers to kids, very good. Shortly after, Larry left to take a teaching job in the area. We raised up a woman to run the children's ministry who had been active in it. She was soon overwhelmed by the task and resigned. We panicked. Where could we find a qualified children's pastor to oversee this ministry?

I made an off-the-cuff decision that changed my life forever.

With no experience in children's ministry whatsoever, I asked the lead pastor to let me jump in temporarily until he could find someone else. I would hold it together until the church could find and hire a real children's pastor. I couldn't bear to see it fall apart.

I pulled together a small team of workers who were spectacular. I will always be indebted to them for helping me survive my first experience as a children's pastor.

We transformed the children's church room into a country/hillbilly theme. I was too stupid and inexperienced to know that kids don't think hillbillies are cool. What can I say? I am from Kentucky. It was a cheap, fast way to bring some personality to our ministry to kids.

We developed our cast of characters: Uncle Hershel, Betty Lou, Earl, Daisy and others. The volunteers who played our quirky characters were amazing, faithful and gifted.

I slowly began to realize that I wasn't hearing much about how the search was going for a new children's pastor. It soon dawned on me: the pastor wasn't looking for anyone else. This was my new, permanent ministry!

OLD TRACK	NEW TRACK
adults	kids
more respect	less respect
on platform	side room
ministry	child care (?)
main service	kids church
sermons	lessons
padded seats	metal chairs

I was tricked. Kinda tricked. I did volunteer to lead the children's ministry but under the belief that it was only temporary. Now I realized I was stuck. This was my new, permanent role. How did this happen? I got into children's ministry because I thought it was only short term. I later discovered this is how most people get into children's ministry.

I had no idea what my new role would bring my way. No idea!

KidMin Shock

The children's ministry track was nothing like the adult ministry track. I thought ministry to kids would be like ministering to small adults. Wrong.

Where's Larry?

My first Sunday leading children's church could have gone a little better.

The first kid who entered children's church sat down on the

113

front row, looked up at me and demanded to know, "Who are you?" "I'm Pastor Roger," I replied trying to muster some dignity. "Where is Brother Larry?" the kid asked. "He's not here any more," I said. "Well, we don't want you," he announced. "We want Brother Larry." He marched out of the room.

Before I could gather my shredded ego off the floor, I realized I just let my first kid leave children's church unattended. His mother returned with him a few minutes later with that look that said, "You let my kid escape. Don't let it happen again." No one told me I needed to secure the perimeter.

I pulled myself together, tried to muster some sense of dignity and prepared to preach the Word of God to these elementary age barbarians.

The learning curve was steep.

My First Disturbance

A few weeks later and shortly into my sermon, I noticed a disturbance brewing to my right. Relieved to see one of my trusty workers making his way to the scene, I continued my discourse. The disturbance grew. I then caught two more workers making their way to the disturbance area. The chatter grew. Perturbed, I stopped and asked, "What is the problem?"

Without seeing the absurdity in it, one of my workers spoke up and said, "Well, Billy took Bobby's offering money because last week Bobby took Billy's Bible." He looked at me as though I should think all this was reasonable. I ordered the Bible returned, shook my head and picked up where I left off.

That never happened to me in adult ministry. I cannot remember a time when Mrs. Jensen got into a scuffle with Mr. Adams because he took her offering money.

Unlike adults, kids were not willing to sit quietly once I lost their attention. They let me know if my lesson wasn't working out.

Ran Out of Ritalin

Several weeks later I was about to begin children's church when Chris entered the room. He was wired that day. He did not respond to my normal corralling techniques. I stooped down to his level and ask him what was going on with him. He immediately calmed down, looked me square in the eye and said, "We ran out of Ritalin." It was his way of saying that this is what you get when I am not medicated.

Children's ministry. Sigh.

Jim and Willie in Miami

I was struggling with the fact I had transitioned (got thrown) into children's ministry. Children's ministry had always seemed like a lower level of ministry. Adult ministry seemed more worthy, more substantive, more...godly.

> **I had been seduced into believing the great myth of modern ministry: adults are where the kingdom action is.**
> --George Barna

What had happened to me? I used to be a Lead Pastor. Then I was an Associate Pastor. Now I was a Children's Pastor. I was doing this all backwards. How did it happen? Nobody goes from Lead Pastor to Associate Pastor to Children's Pastor.

To my utter amazement I discovered that Children's Pastors have conferences! I didn't even know that. I heard Willie George and Jim Wideman were doing a one-day conference in Miami, FL. I took several of my key leaders, and off we went.

I can't exactly remember who said what, but Jim and Willie taught some stuff that solidified my transition. I knew after that conference I would not go back to adult ministry. My transition was complete.

They taught that Jesus had a children's ministry. That knocked my socks off. All of the Gospels, but primarily Matthew, talk about Jesus directly ministering to children in much the same way He ministered to adults. My mouth dropped open. I had never thought about that. They quoted scriptures that made it clear.

> *Then people brought little children to Jesus for him to place his hands on them and pray for them. But the disciples rebuked them. Jesus said, "Let the little children come to me, and do not hinder them, for the kingdom of heaven belongs to such as these."* (Matthew 19:13,14 NKJV)

> *People were bringing little children to Jesus for him to place his hands on them, but the disciples rebuked them. When Jesus saw this, he was indignant. He said to them, "Let the little children come to me, and do not hinder them, for the kingdom of God belongs to such as these.* (Mark 10:13,14 NKJV)

> *And he took the children in his arms, placed his hands on them and blessed them.* (Mark 10:16 NKJV)

> *But Jesus called the children to him and said, "Let the little children come to me, and do not hinder them, for the kingdom of God belongs to such as these.* (Luke 18:16)

And Jesus did all this directly to kids without going through parents. I assume the parents brought the kids and, therefore, approved of Jesus teaching, praying, blessing and laying His hands on them. But He didn't go THROUGH parents to do it.

Jesus also promised the biggest rewards to those who served and ministered to children.

And if anyone gives even a cup of cold water to one of these little ones who is my disciple, truly I tell you, that person will certainly not lose their reward. (Matthew 10:42)

I remember Willie saying that the Greek word for "cold water" meant Koolaid. I never knew that!

"Wow!" I thought, "All I have to do is get the snacks to the kids and I would have a reward that I could not lose." That was stunning to me. I could do that.

I have always been amazed, not only by this promise Jesus made to kidmin, but that He DIDN'T say anything like it to other ministries.

◆He didn't promise ushers anything for getting people to scoot over.

◆He didn't promise greeters anything for getting people to take the bulletin.

◆He didn't promise parking attendants anything for getting people to park next to each other.

◆He didn't promise student ministers anything for keeping kids sober and chaste on ski trips.

◆He DID promised kidmin a secure reward for merely getting refreshments to kids. "I'm in!" I said.

Jesus even gave the biggest warnings to people who mislead kids.

If anyone causes one of these little ones—those who believe in me—to stumble, it would be better for them to have a large millstone hung around their neck and to be drowned in the depths of the sea. (Matthew 18:6)

Serious stuff.

I was beginning to realize that ministry to kids was not second-class ministry. Children's ministry was getting bigger for me. I was finally getting it.

Something seemed to be happening in me. It was like being in a long check out line and suddenly the lane next to you opens up. The light goes on. You move fast.

Trying Stuff

Children's ministry was/is insane. The last thing kids want to do on the weekends after spending all week in school is sit down, listen and learn.

He who tries the most stuff wins.
--Tom Peters

With no experience I had to do a lot of groping in the dark to figure out how to make the ministry effective. My strategy: find out what works by trying stuff, lots of stuff, any stuff.

I have heard that Sam Walton would constantly try new ideas in the early days of Walmart. When it became clear to him that his newest idea was failing miserably, he would scrap it. He would then walk into the office, shrug it off and declare that he was glad he got that dumb idea out of the way.

I was beginning to learn one of the most important lessons of my life: how to fail forward. Being willing to try something with no guarantee of success became my way of life. I learned to embrace, not fear, failure. To me, failure simply meant I found one more way that didn't work.

I was ready to try a lot of stuff to discover what worked best for me. Little by little, failure rolled off of me like water. It had no effect other than something to learn from.

Living Water Church was in what was known in our circles as "revival." That meant lots of new people were coming to church. People were accepting Christ. People got healed. And the services were very long...3 and 4 hours long.

With services lasting so long there was no curriculum available to help engage kids for that length of time. I had to experiment. I had to try things. I had to come up with new ideas weekly.

In a weird way, failure became a normal part of the process of moving forward. I knew a lot of stuff probably wouldn't work. But I also knew I had to try new stuff, new ways of teaching, new ideas. I was determined to be the person who had tried the most stuff in children's ministry...and in the process found some things that worked well.

Those days were difficult. It was a pressure cooker. Few rookie children's pastors have to figure out how to fill 3-4 hours each Sunday morning and then again Sunday night. But the pressure of that challenge served well to later help forge a ninety minute high-energy family event called Kidz Blitz. Making 90 minutes rock was—in many ways—a walk in the park compared to 3-4 hours every single, grueling week.

I was so new to children's ministry that I didn't know it was hard to hold the attention of starving, tired kids until one o'clock, duh. Looking back, I should have fed them. That would have filled 20-30 minutes at least.

Like Babe Ruth, I was willing to strike out a lot to hit a few home runs. A lot of stuff didn't work, but some of it did. Much of the interactive nature of Kidz Blitz grew out of the trial and error of these services.

I began to put my heart and soul into making our children's church a super-cool learning experience for kids. The first thing I did was gather up the best musicians in the church and talk them into leading praise and worship in children's church. These were world-class professional musicians that our church paid to lead praise and worship. I was able to pull some strings so they could sneak out after playing in "big" church.

I knew this would rock. They were awesome. They could play anything...absolutely anything. But the kids couldn't care less. They were bored. And I began to realize why: they didn't want to watch, they wanted to participate. For them, it wasn't about the performance; it was about the participation.

Slowly, I was beginning to understand how kids are wired.

Without having much money to spend, I developed our low budget, hillbilly theme. But even with this lame theme, kids gave us their full attention. That's because everything we did was interactive. Kids participated. They were immersed in the action. They were involved. We never made them feel like spectators. They were full-on participants.

Some interesting things happened along the way that taught me how to connect with large groups of kids.

Daisy

I recruited Linda, a single 30 year old who didn't have kids. She knew nothing about kids or children's ministry. None of the kids even knew who she was. She was perfect.

I gave her a long, blond wig with a complete set of country

attire. She had overalls, a straw hat and flannel shirt.

I was ready to shake things up a little.

Giving her instructions to burst into the room at 11:15, I made it clear I wanted her loud, abrupt and overbearing. With no rehearsal I told her all she had to do was tell me that she was going to the Possum County Fair to enter her rhubarb pie. That's it. Just interrupt whatever else was going on and make it loud.

At 11:15 Sunday morning on the dot, Daisy burst into the room from the back door yelling about how excited she was that she was entering her rhubarb pie in the Possum County Fair. I stopped my lesson. I told her that was wonderful, prayed for her success and sent her on her way. The entire skit lasted less than a minute.

I never introduced her or commented on what happened. It just happened. Fast and hard. Then it was over.

I had been teaching about building each other up, and I was setting the plan for a three part skit with one part each Sunday.

The next week, on my instructions, Daisy entered again without introduction. This time she was not excited, not loud and not happy. I asked her if she won the pie contest. She said no. I asked if she came in second. No again. Third? No. "So what place did you come in?" I asked. "153rd," she replied. "How many were in the contest?" I asked. "153," she replied as she broke down bawling.

We now had to apply what we had been learning about building each other up. I encouraged her and pointed out that her cherry pie was probably her best pie and she should enter that one next time. I told her about another county fair this coming week. She agreed. We prayed for her. She left encouraged.

Next Sunday she blew into the room happy and excited because she came in 3rd. We rejoiced with her.

Daisy was a hit and a great teaching tool. From then on she came in every week. What I didn't expect was for her to become the superstar of children's church. Kids demanded that she come in regularly, even though they only saw her for a moment.

Several months later, I had a problem. Linda informed me that she would be out of town for three weeks to visit her parents in Pennsylvania. No Daisy for three weeks!

I explained to the kids that Daisy was off to another county fair. (If nothing else, you have to be resourceful in children's ministry.) When she didn't return the next week, I told the kids she was lost and we should pray for her safe return.

That week a man approached me in church and told me he was a helicopter mechanic and could get me a helicopter and pilot if I ever needed one. "That's exactly what I need!" I responded.

The next Sunday Daisy was still not home. We prayed for her again. Then I led the kids outside to an area I had roped off. A helicopter made a couple of flybys and then landed in the field close to us. Even the adult service stopped to watch the return of Daisy on closed circuit. The helicopter door flew open. Daisy fell out and ran across the field to us. We hugged her as she told us how she had prayed and the helicopter pilot spotted her and brought her home.

The adults applauded the return of Daisy. Even they got sucked into our fictitious story line.

Big Luke's Riot

I was Bubba McCoy, known commonly as "Pa," loosely modeled after Jed Clampet from the classic TV show "Beverley Hillbillies." But after months of skits with various new characters, I began to get restless. My character, Bubba, had none of the pizzazz of the other characters. Bubba was stable; the other characters were somewhat wacky. Bubba was the maypole the other characters swung around. I wanted to play a more riveting character.

And I had an idea.

I simply developed another character, Big Luke Hatfield, that would come in when Bubba was gone.

So the next Sunday I slipped out and put on a new disguise/costume. With a wild-looking blond wig, a patch over my eye and wearing overalls, Big Luke Hatfield was ready to make his debut.

Without warning, I burst into the room and shouted at the top of my lungs, "Where's Bubba!" Two 6-year old girls ran out of the room screaming. Workers chased after them and calmed them down.

Of course, Bubba wasn't there.

"One of his cows got out and ran over my Mulberry tree!" I angrily proclaimed. "Next week I'm coming back," I said, "You tell him to be here." I then walked over to our general store and stuffed (stole) a few items into my pockets before stomping out of the room.

My plan, I was convinced, would go down in the history of children's ministry as one of the greatest teaching moments ever.

The next week the plan was to enter the room again as a holy terror, looking for Bubba. I would step onto our small stage and ask the workers where he was. They would deny knowing his whereabouts. I would then step off the stage, fall down and pretend to hurt my leg. The workers were instructed to gather around me and pray over my leg. My leg would get healed which would result in softening my heart. They would then share the good news about Jesus and lead me to put my faith in Him. The kids would get to see the Lord reach this crusty old man with the power of the Gospel. What a plan! I knew this would be a blockbuster.

At the right moment, I, dressed as Big Luke, kicked the back door open and entered the room yelling for Bubba. I stuffed another item in my pocket from the general store and walked onto the stage to interrogate the workers about Bubba's location. They said they didn't know where he was. I stepped off the stage, fell down...and never saw coming what happened next.

The first 3 or 4 rows of kids pounced on me. I was already on the floor, so I suppose they figured they could take me. My blond wig flew up in the air. My eye patch came off. I found myself praying that God would spare my life. I didn't want to die in children's church.

I could faintly hear my workers saying as they peeled the kids off of me, "Now this isn't right. We have to go back to our seats." I was in a fetal position when the workers put the wig and eye patch back on me. They stood me up. I mumbled something resembling the sinner's prayer and stumbled out the back door.

What a disaster! Failure is one thing, but starting a mob riot in children's church is another. I was down.

The kids, however, had a blast. They went home telling their parents, "That mean old man came back again this week...but we got him!"

Mr. Wheeler

We had outgrown our children's ministry room so we moved outside into a huge, wedding-size tent. It was Florida. We were hot, but as Floridians, we could take it.

I was learning what all kidmin learn to survive: resourcefulness. That means you use what you have to its full potential. That not only refers to stuff, equipment, etc., but also people.

Troy was a friend of mine who was creative beyond description and, I discovered, did a killer impression of Mr. Haney from the old Green Acres television show. Mr. Haney was a con man who was always trying to sell something to Mr. Douglas, the city slicker living in Green Acres. He was always ripping him off with some deal.

I talked Troy into playing Mr. Wheeler, a local salesman who would try to sell us stuff in children's church. This would be our opportunity to pray for God's guidance about the things Mr. Wheeler was trying to sell us.

The first Sunday Mr. Wheeler entered the tent with an old beat up radio with foil on the antennae. He told us it was a home entertainment center. The boys in the back were screaming, "He's trying to rip you off!" We prayed and then passed on the home entertainment center.

Mr. Wheeler came around every other week.

One week he led a live donkey into the tent and told us it was a thoroughbred race horse whose ears had been elongated for aerodynamic effect. "It's a donkey!" the kids screamed. We prayed. We passed on the race horse, too.

Mr. Wheeler provided a way for us to involve the kids in godly decision making. Even with the obvious, over-the-top humor, they got the point. Troy now works in Hollywood on reality TV shows.

Uncle Hershel's Birthday

People will forgive a lot of mistakes if they like what you are doing.

Our children's church tent was enclosed on one end. The vinyl panels helped keep the wind down while the openness still allowed for a slight breeze.

For some reason, I determined that we were going to celebrate Uncle Hershel's birthday. Uncle Hershel (played by my friend, Gus) was a weekly character in children's church.

> **"All that is not eternal is eternally irrelevant."**
> --C.S. Lewis

I set up a card table in the front corner of the tent. I had a large birthday cake with candles galore to celebrate Uncle Hershel's big day. I realized I was not going to have enough cake to give everyone a piece so I devised a plan. I recruited a "fireman" to help me out by running across the grass and into the tent screaming "fire hazard!" The idea being that Uncle Hershel was so old that all the lit candles on the cake constituted a fire hazard.

I gave the fireman a fire extinguisher from my garage. He had clear instructions to run into the tent screaming "Fire hazard!" and then blast the cake. That would surely make the cake inedible. Problem solved.

As we were singing Happy Birthday to Uncle Hershel, my fireman ran into the tent and executed the plan flawlessly. I, however, did not realize how much power is in a fire extinguisher.

The fireman not only blasted the cake to smithereens, he blew the table away. Yellow sulfur roared out of the fire extinguisher and slammed against the back wall of the tent creating a thick yellow cloud. The sulfur then began drifting over the kids.

I had to evacuate the tent. "Boys, this way!" I pointed. "Girls, that way!" I sent the kids home with yellow sulfur on them that day. "What did you do to my kid?" parents asked. "I shot them with sulfur," I responded.

Parents took it in stride. No one got angry. They liked what we were doing in children's church and were willing to forgive my stupid mistake.

Snoring in Brooklyn

I had heard that Bill Wilson had a massive Sunday School in Brooklyn, NY. It was said to be the biggest children's ministry on the planet. I decided to go there for a weekend and see it for myself.

Bill's story is famous. As a small child, his mother left him on a curb promising to come back for him in 10 minutes. He sat there for three days. A church bus picked him up, and he grew up to become a children's pastor. He eventually moved to Brooklyn to start a Sunday School program for kids, known as Yogi Bear Sunday School.

The ministry was situated in a violent, drug saturated area. It was on Bushwick, the most dangerous street in New York City at that time. When I arrived, my cab driver didn't want to let me out for fear that I would be harmed.

After I settled into a big empty room on the 2nd floor of a warehouse owned by the ministry, a worker handed me a newspaper clipping displaying the stats showing that Bushwick was the #1 place in New York City to get shot and the #3 place to get stabbed. Sweet. I slept on the floor that night behind a steel door and heard shots outside as I fell asleep. There were about 40 other people trying to sleep in the same room. They were also visiting for the weekend, a common occurrence at Yogi Bear. In the dead of the night, I was awakened by a brave nominee who was chosen by my "roommates" to request that I stop snoring. I noticed all 80 glassy eyes waiting for my compliance.

It was typical for them to station visiting ministers on street corners to handout out flyers to children. The next day the other ministers and I were sent out with a thick stack of flyers announcing what would happen that weekend for kids at Yogi Bear Sunday School. They told me say "Yogi Bear" so kids would take my flyers. When the kids poured out of school, I couldn't give away my flyers. They didn't want them. So I cleared my throat and proclaimed the magic words "Yogi Bear!" Kids thronged me, and I gave away all the flyers in a few moments.

Yogi Bear Sunday School had become a trusted name in that battered section of town. Kids liked what the ministry was doing. They connected with it. To them Yogi Bear was not a cartoon character, it was a safe place to be loved.

The ministry was reaching 20,000 kids on a weekly basis. Not bad. Most of them came to their Saturday Sunday School. I saw thousands of kids, including a gymnasium full of preschoolers, learning about Jesus. The sheer volume of kids got my attention.

I went with the Yogi Bear crew to conduct Sidewalk Sunday

School in China Town. I watched in amazement as a big, yellow truck pulled in. The side of the truck folded down making a stage. Suddenly, scores of Chinese kids appeared from nowhere and sat down in rows to watch the presentation about Jesus. It was remarkable.

Wilson's ministry was simple. Love kids. Teach them about Jesus. And play a lot of games. That caught my attention and reaffirmed what I was already learning: kids want to do stuff.

Learn by Doing

My whole philosophy of children's ministry began to evolve toward using participation as my central teaching technique. I created learning experiences instead of teaching lessons. Doing, not watching, became the focus. My objective was to turn every kid from a spectator into a participant. I wanted learning to be so much fun, kids would never realize they got the message.

God never designed learning to be a stale classroom/chalkboard drudgery. He meant it to be an experience. That's the way people in the Bible learned. That's the way Jesus taught. He involved the disciples in everything He did.

I gave up trying to put on a show for kids to watch as I began to realize it was not about my performance, but about their participation. Instead, I committed to finding ways to get kids involved.

A variation on this old saying became my standard.

Tell me and I will forget
Show me and I might remember
Involve me and I will get it

I get criticized for down playing the impact of multi-media

in children's ministry. It is tragic when churches repeatedly sit kids in front of a video, turning them into spectators and using it as a primary teaching tool. No curriculum publisher will ever be able to produce videos that compare with what comes out of Hollywood. We will never keep up with secular video production. Videos work well in short spurts to supplement our message, but on a sustained level.

Only participation can make a kid light up on the inside. Kids are wired for action.

My never-ending quest became finding ways to DO things that would create a learning experience. I used everything imaginable to teach, but games became my method of choice.

VBS Huh?

A few weeks later in May someone asked me whether we were going to do VBS this summer. I had never thought about it. I was new to this children's ministry gig, remember? It had never crossed my mind that parents would be expecting a VBS program. "Sure!" I responded, "You'll be hearing about it."

I had no idea what I was going to do. I just knew I wasn't going to do a traditional, run-of-the-mill VBS. I couldn't see running a cutesy summer program with no energy or relevance.

Having only been in children's ministry for a few months, I was beginning to realize that kids wanted participation more than anything. They wanted to be involved. They wanted to DO, not watch. They wanted to be participants, not spectators. So that's how I designed VBS.

We turned the main auditorium into a place where I led them in the most high-energy, stage games I could dream up. That was really the beginning of the Kidz Blitz format, blending games with content. I don't remember what we called it then, but it was a hit.

The games were not only fun to play but also to watch. I remember we played a game where we fed two kids (one from each team) a mouth full of watermelon complete with seeds. They ran around the auditorium trying to swallow the melon without swallowing any seeds. When they reached the stage they spit out what was left into separate bowls. The winner was the team with the most seeds in their bowl.

The kids lit up. They got to be a part of something they had never seen before. It was fun to play. Funny to watch. They were completely engaged...and learning. It beat every other teaching method I tried.

The game helped me illustrate the importance of taking in the good stuff (God's Word as represented by the melon) and spitting out the bad stuff (ungodly ideas as represented by the seeds).

We had a lot of fun and the kids learned a few things.

Kids loved the interaction, energy, music and fun games. And I began to get a revelation: kids learn BEST by doing. That's the secret! It's not about putting on a show, it's about creating an environment where kids can learn by participating.

Beyond Behavior Modification

Now this is eternal life: that they know you, the only true God, and Jesus Christ, whom you have sent. (John 17:3 NKJV)

His divine power has given to us all things that pertain to life and godliness, through the knowledge of Him who called us by glory and virtue, (2 Peter 1:3 NKJV)

One night, recently, I was gassing up my car when my cell phone text messaging started to heat up. It was a well known minister mad at me over a blog I had written. I apologized and asked him what blog had offended him. It was the one on values/virtues.

I had blogged about the fact I was not a fan of focusing children's ministry content on teaching values and virtues. I expressed my viewpoint (passionately) about the power of connecting kids with Jesus and the folly of focusing on behavior. Evidently, there are some who disagree!

As Kidz Blitz developed, my heart's desire began to come into focus: to use participation to show kids/parents what God is like. That became the heart and soul of the ministry God was preparing for me.

Many people know inside that they are sinners. They know they aren't right. They know a lot about right and wrong. What they don't know is what God is like and how Jesus relates to their lives.

For many, their picture of God is someone who is distant, uninvolved, and judgmental. They don't grasp how Jesus changes all that. They don't understand what God did for them in Jesus. They don't understand God's love, faithfulness and power. Knowing what God is like changes everything.

Life is not about values and virtues. It's not about church. It's not about social justice. It's not about anything you do for God. It's about knowing Him and that starts with receiving Jesus and learning what God is like, really like.

I just think kids/parents/people need to know that Jesus is worth having in your life. He is faithful, powerful, consistent, involved and down right committed to you. Miss that little piece of info and everything else becomes a blur. Christ is the center of our life, message and ministry.

Knowing Him, and what He is like, makes a difference. It is

tragic when Christianity down plays relationship with Jesus and is dumbed down to mere behavior modification. Our message—like Jesus—is alive and dynamic. It helps when we remember that.

Grasshopper Brain

Jumping tracks takes courage. Plain and simple courage. Staying on the track is usually safer than jumping off. We instinctively know that. And sometimes I feel pushed off the track, which makes it easier to change directions. But often it just takes the boldness to jump.

We often treat courage as a kind of optional feature of our faith, but it is a central dynamic in the Bible. Courage is often a Biblical command. God PROMISED the Israelites a special place to live: the promise land. All they had to do was go get it, march in there and take it. Instead, they sent spies to make sure it was safe.

Ten of the twelve spies that returned after sneaking around in the promise land brought back a dismal report. Only Joshua and Caleb were ready to take action. The rest were not.

They had a grasshopper mentality. They saw themselves as puny compared to the enemy. They failed to factor in God. Mistake.

> *Then Caleb quieted the people before Moses, and said, "Let us go up at once and take possession, for we are well able to overcome it." But the men who had gone up with him said, "We are not able to go up against the people, for they are stronger than we." And they gave the children of Israel a bad report of the land which they had spied out, saying, "The land through which we have gone as spies is a land that*

devours its inhabitants, and all the people whom we saw in it are men of great stature. There we saw the giants (the descendants of Anak came from the giants); and we were like GRASSHOPPERS in our own sight, and so we were in their sight."(Number 13:30-33 NKJV)

The ten spies ruled the day and talked the nation out of jumping the track from the wilderness to the promise land. Consequently, the Israelites stayed on their wilderness track for 40 years. In an area that they could have marched straight through in three days, they scooted around in for the next 40 years. Let that sink in. Their fear kept them on a track that went around in circles.

Grasshopper brain never wants to jump tracks, never wants to take risks, never wants to move away from what is safe and secure. And the truth is this: grasshopper brain makes sense. The ten spies were right! The enemy WAS bigger. The spies made perfect sense to the entire nation. Only Joshua and Caleb saw the fallacy of their fear. And that is the problem: jumping the track is not always the sensible thing to do. But it is often the courageous/faith thing to do, and God honors bold faith when it follows His leading.

When God turned over the leadership reigns to Joshua, God talked to him about courage. After 40 years of stomping around in the woods, the people were ready to possess what God had promised them. That's an amazing concept. The people had a promise land from God, yet they had to "possess" it; they had to put their foot on it. The promise land was not coming to them. They had to go to it. They would only realize the promise if they moved forward in courage. God's promises are not automatic. We have to put our foot on them, believe them and act on them for ourselves.

Every place that the SOLE OF YOUR FOOT WILL TREAD upon I have given you, as I said to Moses. (Joshua 1:3 NKJV)

Have I not commanded you? Be strong and of good courage; do not be afraid, nor be dismayed, for the LORD your God is with you wherever you go. (Joshua 1:9 NKJV)

After 40 years the Israelites had conquered their grasshopper brain mentality and were ready to jump tracks. When they did, God took them to amazing places and showed them amazing victories. The Israelites still had issues to resolve, but it beat being lost in the woods.

Similarly, we were to the point in our lives where we were ready to enter a new faze. We knew our time was up at the church in Tampa, and it was as if God had lifted the peace from our hearts. I was eager to see whether or not this interactive style of ministry that works so well with kids in my children's church would also work with families of other churches. Could I make this into an event that churches would host? Could I pack enough equipment into my Aerostar minivan, travel to different locations, set my equipment up on different sizes of stages and conduct a cool event for parents and kids? Would churches from different denominations invite me to come? The details were overwhelming.

My grasshopper brain resisted. It said, "What are you going to do? How are you going to pay the bills? Where are you going to live? What will your friends and family think? Are you just crazy?"

Everyone has a grasshopper in their brain. Mine told me I couldn't develop a family event cool enough for churches to want it or pay for it. It told me I was not creative enough. It told me I was doing all this for myself and not God. It told me everything imaginable except what God could do. Grasshopper brain always leaves out God.

I was considering the biggest track jump of my life. And my grasshopper was going wild. And for good reason.

I have a Secret

Recently, someone wrote a scathing blog in which he said that the kidmin gurus do not impress or help him. He specifically said that he was tired of the gurus who "shaved their heads, had a goatee, used Mac computers and went to Starbucks." Whew. I don't go to Starbucks. There for a minute I thought he was talking about me.

But I know this. I am not a kidmin guru, at least not in the sense of being someone that children's pastors should go to for broad children's ministry guidance. Why? Two reasons. One, I never built a rocking children's ministry from scratch. Two, I was a children's pastor for only a year when I started Kidz Blitz. There, I said it. I took over as children's pastor and started Kidz Blitz a year later. So my experience in running a children's ministry is limited.

So, if you are looking to me for overall children's ministry guidance, you might want to go ahead and start thinking about changing careers. I have been in ministry for over thirty years, but only a fraction of that was in children's ministry at a church. I am not your go to guy for all things kidmin.

I know a few things about ministry in general: creativity, theology, participation. But I am not an expert on the broad spectrum of everything it takes to make a children's ministry effective. That's why I don't write on many kidmin topics. It's not that I haven't gotten around to it. It's because I don't know enough to comment. Please call the paramedics if you ever see me writing articles about preschool ministry, nursery, organization, budgeting, bus ministry or special needs ministry. It means I have lost my mind.

I was never an expert in children's ministry. All I did was jump the track into an opportunity God presented. And the next jump was the biggest.

Jumping the Status Quo Track

Doing the Unconventional

Craziest Jump Yet

Until this point, traveling children's ministries were dominated by puppets, magic, jugglers and clowns. That was the status quo. It was talent-driven. Children's evangelists would build their ministries based on their unique ability to entertain kids. And they were good at what they did. My vision was something different, something that hadn't been done before.

The other times I jumped the track I was jumping into something defined, a path already traveled before. Others fight shyness. Others change beliefs. Others move out of state. Others change ministries/careers. This next jump was going to be different. There was no pattern to observe, no other ministry to glean

"If at first an idea is not absurd, then there is no hope for it."
--Albert Einstein

from. This was a free-wheeling, fly-by-the-seat-of-my-pants endeavor. I was about to start a ministry that did not have a clear model.

I desperately wanted to see if the same type of high-energy, interactive teaching approach I was using with the kids at Living Water Church would work with families. Could parents and kids under 12, share a super-cool experience in a one night event in church that would bring them together and uplift Jesus?

Would it work? Not knowing the answer to that question tormented me. I was afraid not to try. I wasn't sure I could live with the regret of never giving it a shot. I had to know.

I was afraid of coming to the end of my life only to realize I

140

missed some amazing opportunities because I was too afraid to risk failure, too afraid to try. My fear is not failure. It is regret, not the regret of things I did but the regret of things I didn't do.

Progress is about replacing the fear of change with the fear of mediocrity, being more afraid of missing something remarkable than of failing. It is about being afraid of arriving at the end of life's journey only to realize you could have done so much more if you had taken a few more steps into the unknown.

I don't want God to say to me one day, "I was ready to do a lot more through you on earth, but I couldn't get you to try anything different." I don't want God to have to work overtime to get me moving. I would rather have Him work overtime to slow me down or stop me.

OLD TRACK	NEW TRACK
support staff	no staff
stable salary	no salary
stability	instability
smart plan	making it up
at home	on the road
predictability	surprises
tolerable	rewarding

The time had come to move on. With our commitment to the new direction God was leading us in, we asked Him for the money to move ahead. A short time later, Charles, a friend from church, took me out to lunch. Charles was a successful business man in the construction industry. We had a nice lunch and talked about nothing in particular. At the end of lunch, Charles did something unexpected for no specific reason other than he felt God wanted him to do it. He gave me a check for $5000. I was taken back. That was our confirmation that the time was right to jump track. Tammie and I knew it was time to resign from the church and start a new kind of kids/family ministry.

We called this new track "Kidz Blitz."

We used the money to buy some of the stage equipment and props that I had envisioned and had not yet put into reality. The creations came quickly. The money went fast.

Another friend of mine, Carl Perry, who was part of the original church we started in Tampa, loaned me $10,000 to buy additional equipment and supplies and provide for living expenses. Carl waited patiently and allowed us to pay back the money as we were able. It is embarrassing to say it took 8 years!

I took the seats out of my Aerostar minivan and packed it to the roof with quirky equipment. How many minivans were on the road packed with wooden barrels, foggers, hula hoops, colored lights, a 5' tall weigh scale, flippers, a treasure chest and a large wooden mallet? And, 10' sections of PVC pipe strapped to the top of the van. Every time I hit the brake, I was afraid it would all slam into the back of my head or sail off the roof into the car in front of me. I looked like Fred Sanford with a traveling ministry.

I was ready to go. No church backing me. No income. A wife, four kids, and a God prompting me to show the world, or at least where ever my minivan could go, a way to involve kids in the gospel of Jesus Christ. I would go anywhere invited. If you had a zip code...I was there.

The First Season

Where do you go with a new idea and a loaded minivan? We found out there are churches out there willing to be a guinea pig. Well, they might not have known I was experimenting on them. I may not have been clear about that.

Leon Van Rooyen, a South African evangelist who had been on staff with me at Living Water Church, set me up with some churches in Illinois. Ken Dovey, who is now on staff with Kidz Blitz, helped get us an event in his church in Indiana. I was getting a chance to try things out and see what would work.

That first year, starting in October of 1996, Kidz Blitz criss-crossed the eastern part of the United states with fervor and excitement. With the minivan loaded and no room for the whole family, Tammie stayed behind with the kids. I took at least one of the two older girls with me on every trip, often for weeks at a time.

Breaking the Rules

I didn't have any money to advertise. No magazine ads. No mailing list. It was 1996; my only recourse was to learn how the web worked and use it to get the word out about what we were doing. And I did. Churches began to find Kidz Blitz on-line. It was different back then, but I learned what to do and what not to do. I read everything about the web I could get my hands on. It was either learn the internet or drown.

The timing was perfect. The web was just beginning to be a source that churches looked to. If I had started a year earli-er, it would have been much harder to get Kidz Blitz off the ground.

We broke the rules. Back then everything in children's minis-try had either puppets, clowns or magic. We had none. With-out any of the expected acts, we were an oddity in children's ministry. Some churches told us they brought us in just to see what was left when you take out puppet, clowns and magic.

But churches began to call. Requests for Kidz Blitz began com-ing in almost daily. No one was more surprised than me.

Later, as technology improved, I was pressured to incorporate multimedia. That was the trend. Everything was moving toward video, Power Point and video graphics. I just wasn't impressed. People criticize me for this opinion but I am not a fan of ANYTHING, including multimedia, that turns kids into spectators. There are ways in children's church to use multimedia to enhance the interaction but even that is not my style for Kidz Blitz Live. Pure, raw, high-octane interaction drives this event. I was, still am, resistant to anything that weakens this strategy.

Sometimes the smartest thing I did was to figure out which direction everything was going and drive full speed in the opposite direction.

Bias for Action

I developed a passion for taking imperfect action, trying stuff that might work but would probably fail. I often made it up as I went and learned from the experience. I have a bias for action. That means I would rather err on the side of doing something wrong than on doing nothing at all.

"We should be taught not to wait for inspiration to start a thing. Action always generates inspiration. Inspiration seldom generates action ."
--Frank Tibolt

However, there is a fine, but critical, line between having a reckless attitude and having a bias for action. You must be able to make the distinction. Recklessness is taking action without regard to the outcome. Having a bias for action means weighing the consequences, praying for clarity and then stepping into the unknown. It means you know the risk but are willing to take it.

Fear paralyzes. Recklessness destroys. Taking action when the results are still unknown often opens doors of opportunity that would have otherwise been closed.

We do this every day when we drive a car. Sitting at home is safer than driving. Reckless driving will put you in the hospital or the morgue. Taking the simple step of turning on the ignition and backing out of the driveway is risky…always risky. But we do it everyday. Why? Because in our world, it is the best way to get from point A to point B.

The same is true for life itself. You have to back out of the driveway of what is familiar/safe if you ever hope to get anywhere exciting.

Add faith in God to that equation. Pray. Read the word. Trust God. Listen. Then back out of the driveway. The possibilities of what might happen are endless.

Revel in the Mess

Ministry is a lot of things, tidy is not one of them. It messes with your plans, your family, your relationships, your time, your mind. It even messes with your faith. There is nothing about ministry that is safe, predictable or orderly.

> *Where no oxen are, the trough is clean; But much increase comes by the strength of an ox.* (Proverbs 14:4 NKJV)

Got oxen? If you have a strong beast that can pull a load, you also have a mess. Want a clean trough? Get rid of the ox. I don't have an ox, but I have 6 horses. My wife enjoys riding them. They are strong animals that can carry you along a trail for miles. They are also a pain in the backside. They poop all over the field and barn. They chew up my fence. They even like to roll in mud. They are strong and messy.

Ministry is a little/lot like that. It has power to impact people. It changes what they do, think and say. But it ain't pretty. It is strong and messy. Sometimes more messy than strong.

When God first called me to do ministry, He left out a lot of details. Maybe He thought I wouldn't do it if I knew how messy it would be. He was right. I wouldn't have. I had a rosy picture of what ministry would be.

Upon graduating from Bible college I thought ministry would go something like this: I thought I would pastor a small church that would grow into a mega church within a few years leaving other pastors to wonder how I did it. I expected my wife and kids to be a glorious example of what a happy, flawless, godly family should be. I assumed we would have all major theological issues solved. I imagined having a world-class staff that thought I was the best pastor in the world to work under. I anticipated a long, uninterrupted pattern of success, victory and peace. Smooth sailing.

Well, It didn't happen exactly like that. It didn't even happen remotely like that. It has been — and continues to be — a thrilling ride. But it has been messy.

So I like the Proverbs 14:4 verse. It allows me to revel in the mess.

Leaving Florida

In the summer of '97, Tammie found herself at home with the children for weeks on end trying to pay the bills with the small amounts of money I would bring home. The money was like the manna in the wilderness, it was always there. We can't document where it came from, but our needs were

146

being met.

My wife has always been a giver. Giving is not an option to her. You give what you have, and God takes care of the rest. If she sees a need, she is right there with whatever she can offer even if it is not much. She has always stressed that tithing is not an option either. Ten percent of every dollar belongs to God. She takes literally the scripture that says, "Give and it will be given to you, pressed down, shaken together, and running over." From the beginning of Kidz Blitz, this was her mind set. Kidz Blitz tithed. Money was always there when we needed it. That doesn't mean we didn't get behind on bills. We did!

That summer it became obvious that living in Florida was not practical for what we were doing. With the call to travel all over America, we needed to be more centrally located. We put our house up for sale. The house payment was one of those bills that had gotten behind. We needed the house to sell, and two weeks before foreclosure, it sold. We didn't make a profit on it, but we didn't lose money either. We don't understand why things go until the last minute to be resolved, but we don't have to understand. We just praise God for the result.

We were now a family of six without a home! We had a storage building full of the important "stuff," a Mazda 626 and a minivan packed with Kidz Blitz. And, enough events booked to put us on the road for two months. We caravanned from the end of September until Thanksgiving. Some in my family called us gypsies. That angered me. We weren't living outside of town in a covered wagon.

The girls kept maps so they could put stickers on the states they went through. At 3 years old, Morgan could boast of the 15 states she had traveled. The girls had lots of life experiences.

We spent the last six weeks of 1997 in a rented two bedroom apartment in a rough section of Tampa. A friend owned it and gave us a deal. I am trying to think of a good way to describe our humble abode. One good thing to say is that we were all in one place. Very snug together in one place, a very small place! We had one bed, a fold out couch, a small crib for Morgan, and a small mattress in the closet for Shannon. We learned to be happy no matter where we were and no matter how many Palmetto Bugs ventured into our kitchen in the middle of the night.

After the Christmas of 1997 we took ourselves and everything we owned and moved to Kentucky. Lexington that is. My hometown, where I grew up. We were now in a central location, the intersection of I-75 and I-64 where traveling would keep me a little closer to home.

The Secret of the Tishbite

Now Elijah the Tishbite, from Tishbe in Gilead, said to Ahab, "As the LORD, the God of Israel, lives, whom I serve, there will be neither dew nor rain in the next few years except at my word. (1 Kings 17:1 NKJV)

As amazing as Elijah was, he fell prey to the Broom Tree Syndrome and it almost killed him, literally. The Broom Tree Syndrome is best described as being paralyzed by depression because of the size of the task ahead. Elijah reminds us that no matter who you are or what you have accomplished, the Broom Tree Syndrome is a real threat.

Elijah was a Tishbite (whatever that is). His accomplishments are impressive.

• Faced down the King.

- Successfully prayed that it wouldn't rain for 3 1/2 years.

- Prayed for rain and it came down and crops grew.

- Saved a woman and her son by miraculously producing flour and oil.

- Raised a widow's dead son to life.

- Called down fire from heaven that burned up everything including a water soaked bull...and the stone altar it was on.

- Slaughtered 400 false prophets of Baal with a sword.

- Out ran the king's chariot on foot.

Elijah the Tishbite would have been a red hot conference speaker. Seriously. Anybody who can bring down fire from Heaven and burn a hole in the ground would be worth seeing. He would be the keynote speaker at Catalyst for sure. Can you imagine his intro? "You might want to move back a few rows for this next speaker. The last time he was here he burned up three rows of chairs, two video monitors and an usher."

The point is Elijah was an amazing character in the Old Testament. Elijah was my kind of prophet/evangelist. He was John the Baptist times ten, not the sissy kind we sometimes see now. He was a tough-as-nails-don't-mess-with-me prophet. He was not—how do we put it now—laid back.

Yet...

He was once so afraid of Jezebel that he ran away, sat under a broom tree and asked God to kill him. In a short time, he went from man of power to suicidal basket case.

Elijah was afraid and ran for his life. When he came to

149

Beersheba in Judah, he left his servant there, while he himself went a day's journey into the wilderness. He came to a broom bush, sat down under it and prayed that he might die. "I have had enough, LORD," he said. "Take my life; I am no better than my ancestors." (1 Kings 19:3,4 NKJV)

Twice an angel had to appear to wake him up and tell him to eat something. Then Elijah walked for forty days to spend the night in a cave on Mt. Horeb. There he was trying to figure out what God was saying to him.

He experienced a strong wind, an earthquake and a fire, but God's voice was not in any of it. Calamity is NOT God's primary way of speaking to us. Then Elijah heard a still, small voice. Finally, God was talking to Elijah and he was listening. Question. What was God's divine revelation to this great man of faith and power in his time of ministerial despair? What profound words did God impart to Elijah? How did God pull Elijah out of his hole of self-pity and defeat?

First, Elijah felt compelled to unload his frustration with God. I get that. I've been there.

He replied, "I have been very zealous for the LORD God Almighty. The Israelites have rejected your covenant, torn down your altars, and put your prophets to death with the sword. I am the only one left, and now they are trying to kill me too." (1 Kings 19:14 NKJV)

Elijah whined about being alone in ministry and his life being threatened even though he was faithful to God. Not fair!

So how does God respond? Was it a revelation of God's love for Elijah? No. Was it a vision of the coming of Christ? No. Was it a fresh anointing of God's Spirit? No.

Are you ready for it?

150

The LORD said to him, "Go back the way you came, and go to the Desert of Damascus. When you get there, anoint Hazael king over Aram. Also, anoint Jehu son of Nimshi king over Israel, and anoint Elisha son of Shaphat from Abel Meholah to succeed you as prophet. (1 Kings 19:15,16 NKJV)

That's it?! That's all?!

Go to Damascus and anoint three people? Are you kidding? Let's see. God's answer to Elijah's whoa-is-me, nobody-likes-me, ministry-isn't-going-like-I-planned, self-pity syndrome is this: God simply told Elijah to take his next step.

That's it. Just move ahead one space. Don't stop. Put one foot in front of the other, and do the next thing God shows you to do.

Oh, there is one more thing God said to Elijah.

Yet I reserve seven thousand in Israel—all whose knees have not bowed down to Baal and whose mouths have not kissed him. (1 Kings 19:18 NKJV)

In other words, it never was as bad as you thought, Elijah.

Those two concepts have sustained me in ministry.

1. Taking the next step.
2. Stop thinking things are worse than they really are.

There you have it! The Tishbite Method for overcoming the Broom Tree Syndrome: small steps forward will keep you from imploding.

I didn't know much, but I knew I had to keep taking steps forward. Faith is a walk. One step, then another. There is no substitute for taking one step at a time. It sounds sappy, but it really is the only way. Some days I take a leap forward; most days I take small steps.

I would often get overwhelmed by the size of the task. Developing a nationwide ministry from nothing weighed heavily on me. I got to the point that I would sit in my office chair almost frozen with a hundred thoughts racing through my head. Nothing I did ever seemed to be enough to get this new ministry up and running.

Then I turned a corner. I took my eyes off the end goal which seemed so far away, and I focused on daily, little steps. My goal everyday was simply to do something/anything that moved the ministry forward. It didn't matter how small, just something. At the end of the day, I felt good about anything I did at all to advance the ministry.

And I prayed.

This simple prayer helped keep me moving forward. Almost everyday I prayed one simple prayer based on 2 Corinthians 12:9, the second part of the verse.

> *Therefore most gladly I will rather boast in my infirmities, that the power of Christ may rest upon me.* (2 Corinthians 12:9b NKJV)

My prayer went something like this, "Lord, I admit I am weak and do not have the ability to be a husband, father, minister or business man."

This simple prayer and taking steps everyday kept me moving forward.

They understood that they have a choice between distinct or extinct.
--Seth Godin

Creativity

My goal was not to be the best at what we did, but to be the only ones who did what we did. Others may emulate our event…and they have. But my focus was to keep Kidz Blitz evolving so that it was always a step ahead.

I have always believed that Kidz Blitz should be as fresh, original and innovative as possible. That's why I stayed away from TV shows and live events that might resemble anything like what I was trying to create. I originally used the term "Nickelodeon-style" to describe our events, but I didn't actually watch the shows. I didn't want to be tempted to duplicate any of their ideas.

My focus everyday was to try to take a new creative step forward. Big step, small step, it didn't matter. To keep moving forward was my passion. Trying stuff became my life.

I heard Jerry Seinfeld make the comment one time, "If something seems familiar, it's the kiss of death." That summed it up for me. I didn't want anyone in the crowd to see a game or challenge and think, "Oh, I've seen that before."

I am not nearly as creative as people often think. Rarely has an idea popped into my head that turned out to be a great Kidz Blitz innovation. The creativity comes from a couple of secrets.

1. Embracing Failure as Part of the Process

I try lots of stuff knowing that most of it will fail, but realizing that SOMETHING will be a hit. It's worth failing multiple times to find that one something. Creativity springs from action.

The critical question for me when I started Kidz Blitz was this: would it be a cool idea if parents and kids could come together in a shared experience and enjoy learning about God? I thought it would be. I was willing to fail since I thought the idea was worth it.

2. Establishing a Critical Environment

I know this flies against prevalent thinking. But if you want to produce any remarkable ideas, the people around you have to be free to criticize you. That doesn't mean you take their criticism to heart, and it doesn't even mean their criticism is valid. But they have to be free to tear up your ideas and tell you what an idiot you are.

That is the fastest way to evaluate an idea. If you can't defend your idea to the people in your organization, then your idea probably won't get traction in the real world. It is important to create an environment where people encourage new ideas but still have the freedom to tear them up. A strange mix but essential.

If the people in your organization are threatened by new ideas, then you won't get many cool ideas. If the people in your organization are afraid to tell you what they really think of your new ideas, then you will get a false sense of the ideas' effectiveness.

At Kidz Blitz most of my ideas get hammered by the staff. They have that freedom. I don't know everything, and they know I don't know everything. Sometimes I try my idea anyway. The staff usually turn out to be right.

You have to try some ideas just to get them out of the way. And while painful, giving those around you the freedom to shoot down your idea can save a lot of time.

The Push Back

I never assumed problems meant I was doing the wrong thing. In fact, they sometimes mean I am doing something right.

Anytime I attempt to move forward, I expect a push back.

Jumping the track put me on bumpy terrain. When I left the track, I began to realize how many rocks are out there waiting to making my journey a jarring one.

Paul knew he had a "great door" that opened to him, but it also came with opposition from people.

> *because a GREAT DOOR for effective work has OPENED to me, and there are many who oppose me.*
> (1 Corinthians 16:9 NKJV)

It was easy for me to assume that I might have missed God's leading whenever we faced a crisis. Bill(s) we couldn't pay. Broken relationships. Life-threatening illness. Theft. And more! Along the way, I learned that problems and open doors often go together. An open door doesn't mean we are stepping into a place with no opposition, it means we are stepping into a place with amazing potential.

Not Everyone Loves Us

If you're remarkable, then it's likely that some people won't like you.
--Seth Godin

I began to realize that anything remarkable is vulnerable to criticism. If I come up with an idea everyone loves and nobody criticizes it, then it is only an "okay" idea at best. However, if someone angrily criticizes my idea, then I know I might be onto something big. Remarkable ideas provoke criticism.

Every cool idea in history and every God idea in the Bible had fierce criticism. The reason is that remarkable ideas always do one thing: challenge the status quo. And the status quo is something people are willing to fight to preserve. That's why it's the "status quo."

The challenge is to differentiate between: criticism resulting from threatening the status quo and legitimate criticism. Believe me...sometimes I did things that deserved to be criticized.

Not everyone has loved Kidz Blitz.

Sword Controversy

For the first four years of Kidz Blitz Live, I used a real sword to illustrate the power of the Word of God. It seemed reasonable to me. After all, the Bible itself uses a sword as an illustration for God's word. The idea is simple. God's word is not a mere book; it is a severe weapon that damages the kingdom of Satan and cuts out unwelcome sectors of our personal lives.

At the end of the program, I split a pineapple from top to bottom with the sword. I wasn't a martial arts expert, but with a little concentration, I could make the blade come down close to the center of the pineapple, thus splitting it in half. When I missed, I simply explained that I wasn't a trained swordsman, and I would try again. After having been embarrassed with the first miss, I was normally accurate with my second attempt.

I searched long and hard for the right sword to use in this illustration. It was important that the sword was authentic to pull this demonstration off. Most swords are made for display, not slicing pineapples in public. These swords don't have strong blades that extend through the handle. Instead, the blades are cheaply bolted to the handle. This means they could easily break on impact.

That's the last thing I needed: the blade breaking off and flying up in the air. So for a while I used a samurai sword because they all had blades that went through the handles. I learned they call this "full tang." All I knew is that the blade wouldn't break off. But I didn't like the appearance, the Ninja look. I wanted something that looked more like a middle eastern sword, one that might have been around when the New Testament writers compared the Word of God to a sword. I found the right sword and bought three. It was a big, fierce-looking medieval sword.

> **"There is no greater gift than a fierce critic."**
> --Tom Peters

Then I began to hear the criticism. A few bloggers didn't like the visual image of using a sword in church. They criticized Kidz Blitz for promoting violence.

I began to wonder whether it was worth using a sword. The image was troubling to some. And although all of the directors were careful, there was always the slight chance that the sword could slip.

Then Chris Williams, our event director from Kansas City, told me something that made my heart skip a beat. He told me that after he set up for the event he went to get the sword out of the trunk. It was missing. A boy found it and hid it. Chris quickly found the boy and retrieved the sword. But that was enough to scare me into dropping the sword routine.

We haven't used a sword since.

Magician Blogger

Then we heard there was a magician blogger who hated us. He started publishing all kinds of articles about how we entertained kids without using the Word of God.

I was stunned. I contacted him to talk about it. He admitted he had never seen an event but got the impression from our promotional videos that we didn't teach during Kidz Blitz.

He made a good point. I hadn't made it clear in our promotional material about the teaching that we weave throughout the event.

It's amazing how sometimes you learn valuable insight from the people who hate you most. Our friends are often too kind to tell us the truth or so supportive they don't see us critically. Enemies are good at seeing it and saying it boldly; they don't care whether or not they hurt our feelings.

Parody Music

I recently received a letter from a pastor in Oklahoma criticizing the parody tunes we use in Kidz Blitz. He was upset that we use hard rock songs whose original lyrics contain references to drugs and sex. He is right. The original lyrics to some of the songs are vulgar. And that's why we changed them.

Interestingly, some of the traditional hymns found in churches for centuries were originally bar tunes. Some of the lyrics in those tunes were not particularly Christ-honoring.

But the primary reason we use these tunes is to capture the attention/imagination of the adults. The more they engage with us throughout the event the more they tune into the Gospel clarification at the end.

I can understand how some might recoil at our choice of music and consider it inappropriate. I just disagree.

Even MTV Got Mad At Us

Shortly after returning home following 9/11, Kidz Blitz got a letter from MTV Networks. It seems they were…perturbed with us.

When we started Kidz Blitz Live there was no good way to describe the event. So in our naive attempt to describe the interactive nature of KBL, we said it was a "Nickelodeon-style" event. We put this term on the web and on some of the early posters. Even though Kidz Blitz is quite distinct from the Nickelodeon shows (Double-Dare, etc.), it gave us a way to convey the high-energy feel.

It turns out that MTV owns Nickelodeon, and they were not amused that we had used their copyrighted name to describe our Christian event. The letter was dated September 12, 2001. They wrote the letter the day after 9/11. Terrorists destroyed the twin towers, the Pentagon, and an airplane full of brave passengers, killing 3000 people. And MTV was worried about us.

By that time we had already stopped using the phrase, and so we promptly responded back begging for mercy. They let us off the hook.

In those days we didn't think anyone knew we existed. Even as the ministry grew, we often felt overlooked. So to get a letter from MTV was surprising. "MTV feels threatened by us!" I thought, "How cool is that?" We framed the letter and displayed it in the Kidz Blitz office.

2 Battlegrounds

Then I heard a loud voice in heaven say: "Now have come the salvation and the power and the kingdom of our God, and the authority of his Messiah. For the ACCUSER of our brothers and sisters, who accuses them before our God day and night, has been hurled down. (Revelation 22:10 NKJV)

Considering that he is a defeated enemy, I don't concern myself too much with Satan's ability. His power is limited. However, I do acknowledge his keen ability to lie and accuse. He has those maneuvers fine tuned.

There are two areas where Satan had the greatest opportunity to stop me from launching Kidz Blitz. Two battlegrounds where I was vulnerable: ability and motive. I was constantly tempted to question both.

- ◆Do I have enough ability?

- ◆Do I have the right motives?

Anytime Satan can get us to question our abilities and our motives, he can paralyze us. He constantly battered me in those two areas.

First, he tried to convince me that I did not have the ability to create a ministry that would be both effective and financially sustainable. He kept reminding me that most who had tried this before had failed or were still struggling. Actually, Satan was right about this. I didn't have the ability it took to develop this ministry. But this simply kept me in a place of relying on God. I had to depend on Him.

Second, he tried to convince me that my motives are not pure enough. He told me that I was only moving forward for my own benefit. If there is any personal benefit for moving forward, Satan will pour on the guilt.

At first he attacked my ability. When it became clear Kidz Blitz was going to make it, he attacked my motives.

I still battle this.

Wannabes

Kidz Blitz began to look like it might actually survive and become viable. Much to my shock, it became a high-profile ministry. It seemed to have a life of its own. The phone rang multiple times a day from people wanting to book the event we created from scratch.

Despite the increased energy and interest, every year things slowed down in December. I always wondered if the fairy tale was over. Had Kidz Blitz run its course and was now ready for retirement? And every year, just after the holidays, the phone would ring and the emails would again pour in.

Creating Kidz Blitz from nothing and watching it grow was like raising a baby. Even though I knew it was all from God, I still felt like the owner of the ministry God gave me and not a manager of what He entrusted to me. I sometimes felt as though I owned it all to myself.

For this reason, when I saw imitation events starting to pop up, I felt violated. It was as though someone was stealing my baby, something I created and owned.

Ministries appeared that duplicated, not only the style of Kidz Blitz, but photos and exact wording. I was caught off guard. With no thought of the blood, sweat and tears that went into developing KBL, others tried to duplicate its chemistry.

For a few of months I was worked up over this. I even took a pile of printed material from a knockoff event to an attorney. I wanted to know whether or not I had a case. He told me that he thought it was a copyright violation.

I went home and agonized over what to do. I began to realize that my agitation with these other ministries was causing me to lose focus on what was important. I did not have the ability to pursue Kidz Blitz wannabes and continue to advance the ministry God gave us. I had to pick one or the other.

God revealed to me that I was wrong to obsess over what other ministries were doing. He assured me everything would be fine. He would take care of Kidz Blitz. Feeling a bit ashamed of my vindictiveness, I refocused on making Kidz Blitz better than ever.

Later at a conference, a man named Bob approached me, shook my hand and told me how pleased he was to meet me. "Wow!" I thought. "This is flattering."

"I want you to know," he said, "I have copied everything you do and have put together my own kids' event." It was obvious he meant no harm and was only trying to be complimentary. He didn't realize the price I paid to develop Kidz Blitz.

I went back to our conference exhibit and told Ken Dovey, now VP of Kidz Blitz, who I met and what had happened. Ken was already aware that Bob had borrowed ideas from us and was irritated that the man was at the same conference. I told Ken that Bob was really a nice guy and that he should go meet him. At first Ken resisted. Finally, he left the exhibit, met Bob and came back after 20 minutes shaking his head saying, "He is a nice guy."

Today, Bob Herdman, original keyboard player for Audio Adrenaline and author of Christian mega-hit song "Big House" is a great guy and a friend.

I Quit

Contrary to public perception, not everything is fun and games at Kidz Blitz. Not every Monday through Friday is about testing new games and experimenting with cool toys. There have been times I just wanted to quit. Two incidents stand out...

Gone

One morning I came into our office in an industrial district just outside of Lexington. What I saw, or didn't see, knocked the breath out of me.

Our cargo trailer had been stolen. The chain had been cut. The wheel lock had been busted. The trailer was gone and along with it all the stage equipment. The only other Kidz Blitz set was in San Diego.

We did not have the money to purchase enough equipment for another set. The trailer and equipment were not insured for theft. I...was...devastated.

Not only was the loss financially crippling, but my creation was gone. I felt like an artist whose painting had been stolen. It was like multiple hundreds of hours of development, trial/error, sleepless nights were gone. Those thieves had no idea what they had taken from me.

I called the police. They took a report and explained that they would probably never find the set. So I started my own investigation. I went to the neighboring businesses to inquire whether they had seen anything. One had. They saw a suspicious truck with bolt cutters in the truck bed. They wrote down the license number and gave it to me. I was now Columbo.

I took the license number to the Lexington Department of Motor Vehicles and asked the lady at the counter if she would tell me who owned the vehicle. She was appalled at my request and told me it was a felony for her to reveal the owner of the vehicle. I left severely reprimanded.

So I went to the state vehicle office in Frankfort and did the same thing. I laid down the piece of paper with the license number and asked who owned this vehicle. The man looked up at me and said, "It's going to cost you 2 bucks." I agreed to pay, and he gave me a computer print out on the owner of the vehicle. Sometimes, I love government bureaucracies.

I still could not locate the owner. It seems he moved away. Three days later my trailer turned up on the front page of our local newspaper! ATF had busted a ring using my trailer to transport contra band cigarettes.

With article in hand, I went to the federal ATF department in our town. They returned the trailer, but the contents were long gone. Somewhere out there somebody has some strange stuff in their family room.

I was still down about our devastating loss when Karl Bastian, of Kidology fame, put out the word for us about our predicament. Children's ministers everywhere sent money. We replaced the set. I will always appreciate Karl for helping us recover from this "set back."

Flood

A couple of years later, I walked down the office stairs to our workshop in the lower level of the building. I couldn't believe what I saw. The entire basement garage and shop were flooded. Water was two feet deep.

The creek behind the office had backed up and flooded the back parking lot and downstairs. I didn't even notice when I pulled into the front lot.

Lots of equipment got destroyed. While insurance covered much of it, I spent weeks rebuilding props, cleaning tools and drying the floor. Not fun.

Oh, The Places I've Been

The variety of churches that have booked Kidz Blitz Live astounds me. When I started traveling I had no idea all that was out there.

We have been to small churches, mega churches, rich churches, poor churches, evangelistic churches, pentecostal churches, liberal churches, African-American churches, Chinese churches, urban churches, new churches, old churches, cowboy churches, traditional churches and lots of super-modern-high-tech-hip churches. I have seen it all. In fact, I have learned that the church name is inversely proportional to the size of the church. The longer the name, the smaller the church.

In the early days, I seldom knew much about the church before I arrived to conduct the event. One of my big regrets in life is that I did not start a journal of places where I had been. Honestly, the reason I didn't start a journal is because I was NOT convinced the ministry would survive.

Roodhouse

One of my first recollections was a small church in the tiny town of Roodhouse, Illinois. I conducted an event for them on Sunday morning; then the pastor immediately whisked me away to the local prison where he had me preach to hundreds of men in a security facility. It was amazing to see several hundred men march in, sit down and listen attentively about Jesus.

I learned it's not about size. Some very small churches are doing amazing things to advance the kingdom of God.

Rock Church

Rock Church in Virginia Beach, Virginia was the first well-known church that booked Kidz Blitz Live. I was out-of-my-mind excited. Rock Church was a high-profile church with a large national TV audience. This was my opportunity to test Kidz Blitz in a place that was accustomed to bringing in the biggest and best in ministry.

Tammie and I, with our four girls, made the trip from Tampa to Virginia Beach. We took two vehicles: our Mazda and our Aerostar van dangerously packed with equipment and props.

The stage was the biggest I had ever seen. Our set looked tiny. There was enough space left over to conduct a tractor pull.

In those days we had no set fee for Kidz Blitz Live. We depended on church offerings/donations to cover all travel expenses, overhead and compensation. We depended on the goodwill of the churches to sustain us.

The children's pastor explained that his ushers didn't want to hang around after the event counting money so they insisted on taking it up before. I was unsure. Congregations don't normally give toward something they haven't yet seen.

The event went well. Hundreds of families attended. The crowd participated. The energy level was high. Several dozen kids and parents received Christ.

As we were packing up, he gave me the offering: $157.

I was crushed, so much that I put off telling Tammie as long as I could. The offering didn't pay for a fraction of the travel expenses. Sometimes things fall through the cracks at megachurches. They meant no harm but it was a discouragement of epic proportions.

Soon after we began to set a fee for Kidz Blitz.

One of the pictures taken from that event was a cool picture of a preteen boy standing on his chair cheering. I love that picture. It captured the energy of the event. We still use it to this day. I got so much mileage from that picture that it made up for the small offering. Almost.

Prestonwood

A year or two later we got a call from Prestonwood Baptist in Plano, Texas. Not being a Baptist, I had never heard of the church and knew nothing about it.

According to my map, I saw that the church was supposed to be located on a corner at the intersection where I was, but I couldn't find it. I looked at all the facilities on the three corners that had buildings: no church. (I learned a long time ago that churches can be housed in most any facility from a bowling alley to a bar.)

Then I looked at the corner that

THE OOPS FILES

Mistakes are unavoidable. I had to learn to roll with them, laugh/cry them off and move on.

Trying new stuff made for some "oops" moments. I developed the ability to act unfazed even though inside I was having a heart attack.

Fortunately, we have never had an injury, but there have been plenty of screw-ups like:

• blasting T-shirts out of the T-shirt launcher and getting them stuck in rafters.

• setting off assorted fire alarms.

• kids inadvertently exposing themselves while taking off some piece of gear.

Here is some stuff I wish had gone a little better. Some of my more notable blunders could win awards. Be warned, some are rated PG.

was an open field. Way off in the distance I could see a facility that looked like a university. I drove toward it. Sure enough, it was Prestonwood Baptist, the largest Baptist church in the world.

We set up in a large upstairs room. Just before I started, a woman approached me and introduced herself as Sondra Saunders, the director of the children's ministry at Prestonwood. She was obviously the one in charge. She carried herself with confidence and authority. In a very soft but matter-of-fact way she said, "If this goes well, I will put you on the map." She went on to explain that her recommendation had launched many nationally known ministries.

I didn't know what she would think of Kidz Blitz, so I asked if she would give me honest feedback when I was done. She agreed.

When the event was over I approached her and asked what we could improve on. She looked at me, hesitated and said it was the best event she ever had. "I will put you on the map," she said. From that day on Southern Baptist churches called us to book events.

Sondra brought us back the next year to do a VBS event for 5000 kids. We have been there about 7 times now. Sondra has become a good friend, and I will always appreciate her authenticating us to Baptist churches.

Banned

We started getting invitations from many high-profile churches. One of those was World Changers Church in Atlanta, Georgia where Creflo Dollar is the pastor. We went there twice in two years. Then we never heard from them again.

Word got to me that Pastor Dollar watched our second event from a monitor in his office. I heard he didn't appreciate me smashing a 5lb. bag of grits on his platform. It turns out that he didn't see the humor in it. I understand. Kidz Blitz Live isn't for every church.

We were never allowed back.

700 Club

The 700 Club called about helping them minister to 500 unchurched kids at a Christmas dinner they sponsored each year. The plan was that after the dinner, Pat Robertson would preach to the adults and we would conduct a Kidz Blitz in an adjacent theatre for the kids.

When I got there I was told a rapper would perform before Kidz Blitz. I was skeptical that would work but was in no position to object.

THE OOPS FILE #1

Wrong Girl

Once I picked the wrong girl to play the Flipper Jump game. The game involves a kid jumping rope while wearing scuba flippers. The young girl was excited as she approached the stage. Then my heart sank when I noticed she didn't have any hands. I covered my panic and quickly instructed her to sit on the front row. I selected someone else for the Flipper Jump. The next game didn't require use of hands, so I selected her for it. I almost had a heart attack. Few people noticed what really happened.

The rapper was pretty good, but the kids had no interest. He became so frustrated at their inattention that he resorted to throwing his CDs into the crowd just to maintain some semblance of order. The place was near riot level.

Then they handed it over to me.

I began selecting volunteers to come on stage. Within ten minutes the kids realized they could participate if they tuned in. The crowd turned. They became attentive. We had a great Kidz Blitz Live event. That reinforced my belief that kids are wired to participate, not spectate.

McLean Bible Church

McLean Bible Church, a mega church in McLean, Virginia just outside the Washington D.C. Beltway, booked an event. Again I had never heard of the church before. It sounded small to me so I was surprised when I rolled into a brand new, state-of-the-art facility with the coolest parking garage I had ever seen.

They explained that they had just purchased the building from the National Wildlife Federation. The NWF built the magnificent facility and then sold it under pressure from their constituency. It seems that their environmentally concerned supporters did not like the fact that the NWF had destroyed some primo land in building this. So the church bought it and kept their old facility down the road. When I got there, Pastor Lon Solomon was preaching three Sunday morning messages at both locations, driving back and forth between sermons.

MBC was an all-out evangelistic church, even advertising on the Howard Stern television show. The church also attracted a number of senators and representatives in the U.S. Government. They told me Judge Ken Starr, the prosecutor in the Clinton/Lewinski case, attended there. I was disappointed that I didn't get to meet him.

We had a great event, and I fell in love with the church.

Little did I know that MBC would later hold a special significance for me. It was a few years later that I was conducting an event in North Carolina. I jumped a quick flight home in between events to be with my dad during his heart surgery. I flew back to Lexington on September 10, 2001, and thankfully he came though the surgery well. The next day, I was visiting with my dad as he was recovering. I looked up at the TV and watched as the second airplane hit the World Trade Center. It was 911; America was under attack.

I was one of the first in America to fly after 911. After catching a flight back to North Carolina to finish the tour, I drove through Washington, DC on Sunday, September 17. I stopped to attend nearby McLean Bible Church. Every church was packed that Sunday. MBC was crazy crowded. Squished on all sides, the current of people heading into the auditorium was practically carrying me down the corridor of the church. Then someone bumped me hard. A man put

THE OOPS FILE #2

A Little Too Hot

I once built two 10 inch diameter columns out of thick, industrial PVC. They were eight feet tall and wrapped in commercial rope lighting forming a solid column of light.

They looked cool and lit up the stage, but it turns out that rope lighting heats up, especially when wrapped tightly strand to strand. The first time I used them they got so hot that the PVC pipe melted and folded in half at the exact moment I closed the event, as if it were a grand finale. The audience thought I planned it that way. I never told them any different... until now.

his hand on my shoulder and apologized. It was Judge Starr. I was star-struck (pun intended). I told him I was thrilled to meet him. He told me about Barbara Olsen, a TV commentator friend of his, who died on one of the hijacked flights. I appreciated that he took the time to talk to me on such an emotionally charged day.

Don't Call Us...

About 1998 I was invited to present information about Kidz Blitz to a small conference where children's pastors from large Southern Baptist churches had gathered. About 40 children's pastors attended the event at a hotel in North Carolina.

All but two or three of the children's pastors were ladies who had obviously been leading children's ministries for a very long time. They were properly attired and carried an air of sophistication. They appeared to come from a very traditional perspective of ministry.

The topic of conversation among the group was less than inspiring. Apparently a wooden-puzzle maker in Arkansas was quitting. His puzzles were the 4-5 piece puzzles with the little handles on each puzzle piece. Every preschool ministry has them. Because the puzzle maker was no longer going to make this preschool ministry staple, churches from that point on would only be able to get them in plastic. This was a big deal. Highly disappointing to the conference attendees.

In the midst of this dilemma, it was my turn to present Kidz Blitz. I was nervous and wanted to make a good impression. These were influential churches.

I showed them our 90 second promo video before I talked. When I showed the video, I knew I was done. The looks on their faces were ones of panic. Their facial expressions said, "That will never be allowed in my church." They had no interest in what I had to say. It was clear. Wooden puzzles were acceptable, Kidz Blitz was not. No one there booked an event.

I have never been invited back. That's probably best.

Crossing the Border

How hard can it be to get into Canada? Really?

Victor, a long time friend from Morehead, and I were headed across the Canadian border to Toronto. We were conducting Kidz Blitz Live for a New Years Eve service December 31, 1999. The day before Millennial Eve we pulled into the border crossing station.

Border security took one look at our trailer and sent us to the "clearing house," a little building on the border where they try to figure out why you would ever want to come into Canada. There we waited for an hour with several others.

The first group called forward consisted of three young men. The female officer, looking down at paperwork, asked them if any of them had ever been arrested. "Oh, no," they responded in unison. "Really?" she said as she pointed to one of the young men. "How about you in 1993 down in Louisiana?" They were stunned that she knew about that. "Well...uh... that wasn't my fault," one of them stammered. Busted.

My eyes were wide and my jaw dropped. This is serious stuff here. Canada doesn't mess around.

THE OOPS FILE #3

My $*&% are Hurting

Once I had a boy suspended from the truss in a harness. If the harness is not positioned correctly, it can be... shall we say...uncomfortable for a boy. Just before the game started I heard him exclaim, "My balls are hurting!" To the laughs in the crowd, I reemphasized that this is a FAMILY event and promptly moved on.

After the men left rejected, the officer motioned to a young couple to approach the counter. The officer asked them why they wanted into Canada. "Well," the man explained, "We are going to get married in the states and want to visit her family in Canada first." "Really?" responded the officer. "No you are not. You're going to get married in Canada and live here." Then the officer explained in detail what their real plans were. Busted.

Then she motioned to me. After watching the officer deny admittance to everyone before me, I approached the counter in fear and trembling. I didn't know what I would tell the church if I wasn't allowed to enter their country.

"So why are you coming to Canada?" she asked. I explained that Kidz Blitz is a ministry that conducts high-energy family events and that a church in Toronto had invited us to come. "Aren't there Canadians who can do what you do?" she snapped. "I don't think there are any other Americans who do what we do," I said. She disappeared into the back room. When she emerged, looking at me dead in the eye, she said, "I am going to make you a once in a lifetime exception. If you pay the $250 work permit right now, I will let you into Canada." I paid. She stamped my passport. I went on my way.

I'm thinking Canadian officials don't appreciate Americans coming into their country to take jobs from their citizens.

Will You Marry Me?

Occasionally something super-cool happens at Kidz Blitz Live that catches me off-guard.

I had just finished conducting Kidz Blitz Live at Faith Christian Center in Smyrna, Georgia. Cynthia Jenifer, the children's pastor, was a gracious host and diligent leader. We had met her years earlier at a mega church in Detroit.

At the conclusion of the event, Cynthia told me the Pastor's wife had an announcement to make, so I turned over the microphone to her. The auditorium was packed, and every eye was on her as she began to honor Cynthia for her work at the church. The pastor's wife presented her with a large bouquet of flowers and then signaled the media techs to start the video. The five minute video showed a brief overview of Cynthia's life, including pictures of her parents. Cynthia was overcome with emotion at the display of honor being bestowed on her. The video mentioned that she was waiting for her Boaz, a reference to the fact that Cynthia, an attractive woman, had never married.

THE OOPS FILE #4

I Have to Pee!

Once during a Kidz Blitz event held at a children's ministry conference, a female children's pastor volunteered for a game where she would be suspended from our truss in a harness. After being buckled in safely and hoisted up, she loudly exclaimed for everyone to hear, " I have to pee, really bad!" I expected this from a kid, but a children's pastor? Once the game was over we released her and she dashed from the auditorium. We never saw her again.

Then a tall, handsome man, I soon realized was her boyfriend, came forward to share some words from scripture. He then turned to Cynthia and said that he was ready to take their relationship to the next level. Kneeling in front of her, he pulled a ring from his pocket and asked her simply, "Will you marry me?" Some people in the crowd then lifted large black sings with white letters that read, "Will you marry me?" Amidst tears, excitement and shock, Cynthia said, "Yes." The church went wild.

And my favorite part was that it all happened in front of my Kidz Blitz set!

People

People have made Kidz Blitz what it is. They make me look good. Without question, the coolest, most selfless people in the world are people who serve in children's ministry.

Loose Cannons

I'm not a fan of team players. For most, a team player is someone who agrees with everything I do and just seeks to get along. My chocolate lab, Cookie, can do that. What I need is renegades, crazy people, loose cannons. I like people who have ideas and speak their minds. No one will ever get fired from Kidz Blitz for standing up to me and telling me what they think. I may not agree, but I need different perspectives.

It's the people God brought to us that made Kidz Blitz succeed. People make or break any organization. They are the **"People aren't** most important resource. Anything **everything; they** else can be replaced: buildings, **are all there is."** equipment, etc. With enough alu--Tom Peters minum, antifreeze and positive attitude, even the Green Tornado hour glass, the most stubborn prop I ever built, can be replaced.

Quality people, however, are indispensable. There is no "I" at Kidz Blitz. We are a team, just not a passive team.

We have always kept a lean staff. I don't need a lot of people, just a few people who can do a lot of different things. Everyone who works for Kidz Blitz can do multiple functions. Here are a few of the key players.

Tammie

In the early days Tammie did the bookkeeping. She paid the bills when we had the money. She wrote Critter Land and served as a source for ideas and input. One of the best things Tammie did to help grow the ministry was to insist that we give to other ministries. Even when we did not have enough money to pay our bills, Tammie made sure we gave and let me know it when we didn't.

She was not merely along for the ride. She spoke into the ministry and helped get it up and running. Kidz Blitz would not have launched or survived without her.

Ken Dovey

In 1999 I called Ken Dovey to come help. Ken is brilliant. I worked with him at the early Tampa church. He was the youth pastor there and later hosted one of our early Kidz Blitz events in Indiana.

He has become the point man for Kidz Blitz, explaining to churches about Kidz Blitz Live and our Bible curriculum. Churches contact us every day, and Ken answers their questions. Many call in times of discouragement. Ken listens and offers support. To many he has become a kidmin confidant, someone they can talk to about the challenges they are facing. His daily conversations with kidmin help us stay current with the ever changing world of children's ministry. Ken also makes Kidz Blitz personal. People who call don't merely receive a brochure or catalog in the mail, they talk to a caring, knowledgeable person who can answer their questions. Ken also helps creatively. He co-wrote the lyrics to our parodies and developes ideas for games and challenges.

Ken also speaks up. I tend to be abrasive, so his insight into people helps me relate better. Ken is a better people-person than I will ever be.

Terra Harrison

Shortly before graduating from high school, Terra, my oldest daughter, started working for us. She started out by baby sitting our curriculum-printing, slow-as-Christmas, laser printer. Her organizational skills later freed me up to focus on writing and developing ideas. I never guessed Kidz Blitz would survive long enough for her to later grow into the position of Office Manager.

Terra has a keen eye for graphics and artistic design. She is has strong language skills that help in wording curriculum, letters, mailers, this book, etc.

Ande Long

Ande is the ultimate multi-tasker. She runs our web sites, proofs everything we send out, oversees shipping and even sews fabrics we use in the event sets. Without her this book would never have made it to print.

Kevin Kern

Kevin was an officer in the Navy and the first person other than me to direct Kidz Blitz Live. We conducted events together before I released him to conduct events on his own. I watched him conduct his first event on his own and was so gratified to see that someone else could lead the event I created while maintaining a high level of energy. Kevin directed events from 2000 to 2006 and covered the Western region.

Chris Williams

Mentored under well-known evangelist, Jerry Johnston, Chris was well acquainted with ministry and travel. He was a work horse, traveling several hundred thousand miles across America conducting Kidz Blitz Live events from 2002 to 2009. Chris always carried himself in a way that represented Christ and this ministry with integrity. His home church tried for years to hire him away from us. After Chris got married to Kate and she gave birth to Max, his church finally succeeded in hiring him away. Chris jumped the track and left Kidz Blitz Live to work on staff at his home church. I have not fully forgiven them for taking him from us. But I'm working on it.

Donnie Slade

We got to know Donnie and Christy Slade in the Bahamas on our conference cruise, and he had hosted several Kidz Blitz events at his home church. Donnie jumped the track from his full time ministry position in 2004 to be on the road for us as an event director. Donnie was a people magnet and became an instant hit all over the Southeast. It always irritated me that churches would call us and request Donnie to conduct their events. But plain and simple, Donnie is a great event director. Donnie is off the road now to spend more time with his family.

Greg Baird

Greg is our newest event director, coming on board in 2010. Already well known for his KidMin360 blog, Greg is an established leader in children's ministry. Along with conducting Kidz Blitz Live events, he conducts our newest event, FX Live, a family focused event. Greg covers the Western region and is an ideal addition to Kidz Blitz. We are blessed to have him.

Vomit on the High Seas

Through a conversation with Janie Gausman, owner of childrensministry.net, I was inspired to conduct a kidmin conference on a cruise ship. We booked Royal Caribbean for a four-day cruise scheduled to set sail the next January. We called the sailing conference "Fresh Air."

I thought it would be simple. We secured Jim Wideman, Craig Jutila and Sue Miller to be keynote speakers. Donna Douglas, known for her portrayal of Elly May Clampett in The Beverly Hillbillies, joined us on the cruise as our special guest.

People put down a deposit with us. We reserved the cabins. It was an instant hit. No problem.

Not so fast. Small/big/massive problem. One conference participant (you know who you are) complained because they didn't recognize the name on their credit card statement. So our merchant services company referred us to their fraud department.

They thought we were a fraudulent travel company, so they simply held thousands of dollars in credit/debit card payments. That threw us into a financial crisis of major proportions. Royal Caribbean needed their next payment and our merchant services wouldn't let us have our money. They said they planned to hold it for six months until they were convinced we were legitimate. When they finally released the money to us, they charged us a hefty fee for the service of holding our money. I was mad!

Conducting a conference on a cruise ship turned out to be crazy difficult. When I tried to nail down specifics about multimedia capabilities, conference room availability, etc. I hit a wall every time. It seems that the only people who had the answers I needed was the crew on the ship and — you guessed it — they were always out to sea.

Frustrating. But we pulled it off. Even did it two more times.

One time we got hit by a tropical storm. It delayed us out to sea for a day where we all threw up. Other than that, it was a great bonding time. There is nothing like vomiting with other kidmin to make you feel connected.

We also met some wonderful people including family ministry guru, Reggie Joiner, who spoke for us on the second cruise. We developed many relationships through those cruises. There's nothing like seeing Jim Wideman singing "Sweet Home Alabama" with a German girl on karaoke night.

All in all I am glad we conducted the cruise/conferences but I will NEVER do it again. Ever.

Anything You Want To Do

Jim Wideman, my redneck friend from Alabama, has always encouraged me. I heard him speak in Miami but never got to meet him.

I had heard him speak before, but the first time I actually met Jim I was at the Children's Pastors' Conference in Nashville.

I had just written curriculum and was attempting, without much success, to sell it at my exhibit. Jim came and sat down next to me. "Certain times of the year," he said, "ya just can't give curriculum away."

Since I wasn't selling much curriculum at the time, that comforted me. Jim has been an encouragement to me from that day on. In addition to speaking on all three of our conference/cruises, for two years Jim and I conducted one-day, kidmin workshops all over America.

In my opinion, Jim is the foremost kidmin leader in ministry today. I am blessed that he is my friend.

However...

One time Jim told me that he offered to take his girls (Yancy and Whitney) anywhere in America they wanted to go on their 16th birthday. They could go anywhere; do anything. His girls chose to go shopping somewhere like New York or Los Angeles. It was a special father/daughter bonding time. He encouraged me to do the same.

Shannon, my third oldest girl, was about to turn 16, so I took the advice of my dear friend, Jim Wideman. I told Shannon I would take her anywhere in America to do whatever she wanted to do. "What I would like to do," she replied, "is go to Wyoming and rope a wild Mustang and bring it home."

Shannon, an accomplished horsewoman, thought that would be fun to do. I had to explain that while there are ways we could legally capture a wild mustang, I wasn't sure we would be able to get it into the horse trailer to bring home. She understood and asked to have a day to think about my offer. I agreed.

Realize, I offered her the option of going anywhere in America and doing anything she wanted to do. Anything. She came to me the next day and said, "Daddy, what I really want to do more than anything else is...ride a bull." "Ride a bull?" I responded, "I don't think there is anyplace that will let a 16 year old girl ride a bull."

I was wrong.

It turns out there is a Christian rodeo camp in Maryland that trains girls to ride a bull. Who knew? Plans developed and my wife, Tammie, took Shannon to the week-long, sleep-away camp.

The girls were first trained on a barrel. Finally, they were given a helmet and safety vest as they mounted a real rodeo bull.

Nightly and from the far away comforts of our home, we could log onto the camp website to see pictures posted from each day. Unfortunately, the photos weren't tagged. No names were posted. The first night of camp we saw a photo of a large steer lying on its side. Two legs were protruding out from underneath the steer...wearing Shannon's boots. Since we weren't notified, we assumed she wasn't injured. We had hoped that she would have stayed on the TOP side of the steer.

Before the week was over, Shannon rode three steers and two bulls. One bull ripped the back out of her safety vest. And a steer rolled over on her twice in one day. Some camp workers told her they had never seen that happen before.

On the last night of camp, they held a rodeo. Shannon told them she wanted the meanest bull at the camp. The goal was to stay on the bull for eight seconds. She rode the bull out of the stall and into the rink. The bull jumped and she flew into the air: 1 1/2 seconds.

She came home bruised and banged up and said, "Daddy, it was the most fun I ever had. I want to do it again next year." "I don't think so," I replied. Be careful what you promise your kids.

Jim and I are still friends…but just barely.

Busted

One of our employees here at Kidz Blitz didn't work out so well. We will call him "Bill" (not his real name). Bill not only busted a $3000 monitor at the Children's Pastors' Conference, he also stole from us.

Stuff started turning up missing like a $2500 video camera and then petty cash. We narrowed it down to him or the weird UPS driver. The more we thought about it the more we realized it couldn't be the UPS driver. So we rigged up a motion sensitive video camera over the petty cash drawer. Sure enough, it caught Bill snatching money from the drawer. It was chilling to watch the video and see someone you thought was a friend steal from you. It made the hair on our arms stand up to watch someone we knew and trusted steal from us.

I confronted him. He lied. When I told him I had him on video, he tried to squirm out of it. I fired him. Some people are not what they seem.

Chanley in the Bathroom

One of the most entertaining people to ever travel with me was Michael Chanley, Director of the International Network of Children's Ministry.

Michael is an ex-marine who was on staff at Southeast Christian Church in Louisville, Kentucky. He authored *Collaborate*, a book he compiled with various authors, including myself, contributing thoughts about family ministry. He is now the director of the International Network of Children's Ministries, the parent company of the Children's Pastors' Conference.

Michael is a friend and interesting travel companion. His hobby is texting/tweeting/posting stuff 24/7. He mostly tries to send out stuff to irritate his friends. He gets a real kick out of that.

While the two of us were on the road in Virginia, we stopped at a hotel for the night. Michael attempted to place a phone order with a Pizza Hut that wasn't more than 100 yards from our hotel. When he requested that the pizza be delivered, the request was denied. The pizza employee stated they do not deliver to our hotel location. Michael confirmed that the employee was in fact referring to the hotel that is directly across the street, but the answer was still no.

We then walked to the Pizza Hut and picked up the pizza ourselves. Upon returning to the hotel, we met a Pizza Hut delivery man in the hotel lobby. We asked the delivery man what Pizza Hut he worked at, and he indicated the one across the street. When I asked what he was doing here, the delivery man responded, "We always deliver here." I was left to make the only conclusion possible, Michael had obviously offended the pizza employee causing the employee to deny us delivery. If you can't get Pizza Hut to deliver a pizza across the street, then you need to work on your people skills.

The fun didn't stop there. The next day we stopped at a Citgo gas station. I pumped the gas while Michael took care of nature's call. After filling the tank, I pulled around to the outside restroom to wait for Michael. I noticed huge lettering on the restroom door. It read "DO NOT CLOSE DOOR. IT WILL LOCK YOU IN." I thought that was odd. How do you use a one-seater restroom without closing the door. In this case you would be exposed to street traffic.

Then it hit me. Michael is probably locked in there! At that moment my phone rang. It was Michael. In his military voice he said, "Uh, can you come let me out?" "Sure," I replied.

Then questions raced through my mind. Do I really want to let him out? Would his wife, Rose, want me to let him out? Should I call her and ask? She might be thrilled if I left him in a bathroom in Virginia. If I left him in there, I might be celebrated by kidmin around the world. This could be my chance to make my contribution to children's ministry everywhere. But out of the kindness of my heart, I let him out.

I have always questioned, did I do the right thing? There is just no one I would rather pick on than Michael Chanley.

Family

Juggling a traveling ministry and a growing family turned out to be a little/some/massively harder than I thought.

Officially Disqualified

I always felt somewhat disqualified to lead what became a vast ministry to churches. But it was about to become official.

My family was struggling.

I had put so much time, energy and focus into launching Kidz Blitz that I had made the classic mistake in ministry. I had neglected my family, the one thing I had always said I would never do.

Mica, my second oldest and the one healed as an infant, was rebelling. She lost interest in God. Her friend selection was poor. She fought constantly with Tammie.

About this time, Kidz Blitz was scheduled for our first tour of California. We decided to pack up the whole family and go together. (My oldest, Terra, was in her last year of high school, had a full time summer job and opted to stay home.) Mica decided she wasn't thrilled about spending the summer with the family. The night before we were scheduled to leave, she ran away from home. When we went to her room to wake her up, she was gone. It was one of the lowest points of my life. I was devastated.

One event - Mica running away - was crushing the two things I loved most, my family and my ministry. I felt like my family was falling apart, and if I couldn't make this California tour then Kidz Blitz would crumble. We needed this tour to pay the bills. We needed to leave but couldn't without her.

> "The important work of moving the world forward does not wait to be done by perfect men."
> --George Eliot

I spent the day we were supposed to leave for California searching for my 15 year old daughter. For several hours I called places where I thought she might be. I drove by homes where her friends lived. I prayed. I did everything I knew to do.

I called the police. We didn't know it then, but she was with Allison, an 18 year old friend. Since Mica was under age and with a legal adult, this became a serious legal matter. Then Mica and Allison entered a post office (federal property) making it a federal issue. FBI agents got involved.

Finally, I was able to locate Mica, and after much persuasion, she agreed to come home. She angrily left with us for California. She was not excited about going to the west coast with the family, but she did.

A few days later on the tour, we stopped for the night in Winslow, Arizona, the town made famous in the song "Take It Easy," by the Eagles. There were no vacancies. Every hotel for miles was booked…except one.

Our hotel room was so bug infested, my wife, Tammie, opted to sleep in the van. I was trying to "take it easy" like the song recommended, but it was a struggle.

The three girls slept with their eyes open so as not to miss anything crawling up the walls. By that point, Mica was as scared as she was angry. There is something ominous about spending a miserable night in a town made famous in a popular song. And to make it worse, it was Mica's 16th birthday. There was no party.

It was a rough tour.

Two years later it became clear that Mica had an addiction to drugs. After much denial, she revealed this to a student pastor at the church we attended. They both came to our house where they told me that she had made a decision to try to get accepted at Mercy Ministries, a Nashville ministry that specializes in helping young women.

Desperate for help, I wrote an impassioned letter to Mercy Ministries. Pending drug tests, which she passed, they took her immediately.

I was vaguely familiar with Mercy Ministries. It is located next to Christ Church, a non-denominational mega church in Nashville where I had done two previous Kidz Blitz Live events. Christ Church works closely with Mercy.

We moved her to the dorm at Mercy Ministry. It was hard. I felt like a failure, but I knew this was the best for her. I regretted being away from home so much. I felt guilty. I wished I could do it over. But I couldn't.

Communication while she was there was limited, but we were able to talk with her enough to know that she was making progress. During one of our conversations, she told me that she was working on a project with some of the staff at Christ Church. She innocently made the comment that her dad was Roger Fields. Someone on the church staff heard the comment and expressed astonishment that the president of Kidz Blitz had a daughter at Mercy. "I guess I shouldn't have said that," she told me sheepishly. I assured her it was OK. I realized at that moment how much more important it was to get her help than it was to protect my image/reputation. I didn't care who knew. I was just glad she was getting better.

> **"Sometimes I lie awake at night, and I ask, 'Where have I gone wrong?' Then a voice says to me, 'This is going to take more than one night.'"**
> --Charles Shultz

She came home after a few months. No longer addicted, she began the slow process of navigating her way through life.

On the lighter side (there weren't many during this time), Mica told me while in Nashville she met the coach of the Tennessee Titans, the one who was in charge of the handicapped players. "There are no handicapped players in the NFL," I assured her. "Yes, there are," she said emphatically. "They told me he coached the special teams." I explained that "special teams" meant kickoffs, punt returns, etc., not handicapped.

Today, married with a beautiful little girl, she is a follower of Jesus and an influential TEA Party organizer with a huge political following in Kentucky. And she knows a lot more about football.

She told me something she learned at Mercy that melted my heart. She said, "I found out I had a fairy tale life and never knew it."

I will always cherish those words.

What My Girls Said

Each of my daughters remembers a little differently the travelling during the early days of Kidz Blitz. They were all home-schooled on the highways, in ministers' homes and in hotels for the first year. When we left our position at Living Water Church the girls were also leaving the church's private school they had been attending. Between going to school there and being there for every service, Terra, Mica, Shannon and Morgan were at church every day. That building was a very comfortable place for them. Their school friends were also their church friends. Their teachers were also their youth leaders. Their closest peers were other staff kids. To say they had roots at our home church in Tampa is an understatement. They were buried up to their necks in the church. Anyone might have expected the girls to throw wild and crazy fits when we left, but it wasn't like that at all. God transitioned us in a way that by the time we left we were completely severed from Tampa; there were no longer strings tying them to people or places. We started on this scary adventure as a complete family unit. No one's heart was left behind.

We drove everywhere in 2 vehicles. The Aerostar minivan carried the Kidz Blitz set, me and one daughter. The sliding door didn't have a handle so the passenger always had to open it from the inside. When the whole family did ride together, they joked that one day the door would fly open and we'd lose Morgan. Not very funny really.

Tammie and the other 3 girls would drive behind in a 4-door Mazda. Cell phones existed. But they were the huge, clunky contraptions that cost a fortune, so we didn't have one. Communication on the road is actually what each of the girls remembers most. If someone in Tammie's car needed a bathroom stop, which happened often (they were all girls), they would write a message on a piece of paper, hold it to the windshield and honk until they were sure it got noticed.

Terra, the oldest, spent most of her time drooling over cute boys at every church on the tour. She was at "that age." Back in the minivan, she would write letters to the boy she crushed on at the last stop and then throw them away when she met the next boy. This was before Facebook, thankfully. She made friends with other teens in various cities and often got to see them again on later trips. Terra saw the Empire State Building for the first time from the Aerostar van with PVC strapped to the top.

Guns don't kill people. Dads with pretty daughters kill people. --Unknown

Mica remembers driving all summer without A/C in the minivan. That's why it was more fun and comfortable to ride with mom in the Mazda sedan. At least she played music instead of my talk radio. I didn't realize until later that radios have other stations besides talk. It all came full circle though. Both Terra and Mica only listen to talk radio as adults. Mica's birthday is in July, a good time for booking Kidz Blitz events, so she often spent her birthday in random cities.

Shannon and Morgan had what they considered the most important job of Kidz Blitz. At around 5 and 6 years old, their job was to sit behind the Kidz Blitz backdrop, which in those days was held up with tripods. Their important task was to operate the fog machine and lights. They knew their cues and would sit back there dutifully, chatting like girls do, until time to rotate a stage light or send out a thick cloud of fog. Shannon gave her heart to Jesus at a Kidz Blitz event when she was 8.

The girls never fully adjusted to the biggest trial of travelling, my snoring. Our family of 6 shared hotel rooms when we weren't staying in a pastor's home. The older 2 and sometimes all 4 would sleep in the bathroom, wearing their earplugs. Side note: Terra and Mica did not marry snorers.

Tammie kept the girls interested in anything she could think of on the road: games, books, sights, conversations. If she grumbled or cried for a permanent home, the girls never saw it.

I splurged on my girls any way I could on the road. There was no money for shopping trips or sightseeing between events, but whenever it was time to eat, I would stop at 5 different places for food until everyone had exactly what they wanted. When a gas station bathroom wasn't clean enough for my girls, I drove around until I found a more suitable one.

Terra and Mica's favorite Kidz Blitz trip was to Nassau, Bahamas. Shannon's favorite is a recent one to Florida when she took her best friend Jessie. Morgan's favorite is a family trip to Disney for a kidmin conference where Kidz Blitz was an exhibitor. There were eventually California trips with excursions to Tijuana, the trip to Nassau, Bahamas, multiple Disney and beach trips, Washington DC, New York City, and the list continues.

Princess or Pioneer?

I am a mediocre parent. Should I have spent more time at home? Yes. Should I have been more attentive? Yes. Should

I have been a better listener? Yes. Do I regret being away so much? Yes.

With four girls and a wife, I live in a girl's dormitory. At least it seems that way. Life in an all-female home is…dramatic.

Never having had any sisters I didn't know much/anything about raising girls. Raising kids is the hardest job in world. Period. And girls have their own special set of challenges. There were set backs, but somehow, they have turned out amazing.

Here are three things we did. I'm not saying this is the definitive pattern for raising girls. I am saying this is what we did and somehow it worked for us. Maybe this will help someone else.

1. We tried to raise them with authentic faith in God without using a lot of sappy religious language and meaningless tradition.

2. We gave them room to build their own faith. We wanted their faith to be theirs, not an extension of ours, but theirs.

3. We never over-pampered them. They were raised to be pioneers, not princesses. Today, they are all strong, confident women, a lot like their mom.

Here are our girls starting with the oldest.

TERRA has become the organizational/creative genius that makes Kidz Blitz run. She is off-the-chart creative, smart and much more personable than me. There is nothing she cannot do once she decides to learn how. She is such a great mom she makes me realize how mediocre I was at raising her. If she ever leaves Kidz Blitz, I will probably shut it down and go get a job as a Walmart greeter.

MICA is the political rock star of Kentucky. She is THE voice of the TEA Party in Kentucky and the only person in the state who can hold a political meeting and pack the room. She was featured in USA Today–along with Michelle Bachman and four others–as one of the most influential TEA Party activists in America.

SHANNON is the intellectual bull rider of the family and the only one of the four who ever displayed any interest in sports. At 3 years old, she was watching me channel surf on TV when she blurted out, "Stop! Go back. What was that?" I backed up the channels until she found what caught her attention: a baseball game. She was glued to it. I don't like baseball. None of the others girls cared for baseball or any other sport. Kids are just all different even when you raise them the same. She is now studying criminal law at Eastern Kentucky University on an academic scholarship.

MORGAN loves missions and is already making plans to serve in Belize or some other ministry when she graduates from high school next spring. She has an amazing passion for God and has led many of her friends to the Lord. She is currently working two jobs while keeping up her grades and actively involved in her youth group.

I am a rich man because of my daughters. Period.

...And 15 Years Later

As I write this book, it has been 15 years since Tammie and I launched Kidz Blitz. Today, I am grateful beyond words for the opportunity God has given me to do this. As I began to reflect and run some numbers, I was surprised at what I found:

♦Approximately 50,000 people have made first-time professions of faith in Jesus at Kidz Blitz events.

◆Kidz Blitz events have been seen by hundreds of thousands of people in over 40 denominations.

◆Kidz Blitz has averaged 125 productions per year.

◆Kidz Blitz directors have driven to enough events that the miles added together would circle the globe over 40 times.

And I never set a goal for any of this. All I ever did was jump the track when God said "jump."

Blitz Farm

One day Terra called in sick for work. Tammie headed to her house to help with the kids. She took a country road short cut and passed a farm for sale. The office building on the property caught her eye. We were always on the lookout for a house on property with a commercial building big enough to contain the Kidz Blitz offices and shop. All the properties we had seen before were either too expensive or too far out of town. This one looked promising. She wrote down the number and called me.

I happened to be in a mortgage office co-signing on a small house for Mica, my second oldest daughter. Tammie told me the price. I asked the bank officer in front of me if the bank would finance it. Having just reviewed my finances to approve the loan for Mica, she assured me the bank would go for it.

The farm turned out to be everything, and more, we had ever dreamed of owning. The house was gorgeous. The commercial building had the perfect combination of office space, production area, workshop and garage. The farm had two horse paddocks. Tammie had always dreamed of having horses again. She had horses when she was a teenager.

And on the front of the commercial building was a sign that read "blitz." We looked at that in sheer amazement. An identical sign was also on the front of the barn. I asked the realtor why that was there. He didn't know.

The price was affordable. We learned that it was probably under appraised. We were advised to offer exactly what they were asking. No negotiating. We did. They accepted. The deal was done in days.

We later discovered that the name of the construction company that built the commercial building and the barn was Blitz Construction. They put their name on all their buildings. How about that?

Spirit West Coast

I recently attended a children's ministry conference where they put about 40 resource providers in a small room behind individual tables. We were instructed to explain our ministry to the people who came up to our table. Then they opened the door and we watched 200 people flood in. It was chaotic.

It became impossible to engage anyone in a conversation because of the noise and movement. It was frustrating. After an hour of sheer chaos, the people were herded out of the room. I was packing up and a woman walked up to my table. She told me she wanted to talk to me so she waited for everyone to leave.

She started by saying that 10 years earlier she attended an event in Monterey, CA called "Spirit West Coast." "I know what that is," I said excitedly, "I have been to that too." She knew that already.

Spirit West Coast is a huge annual, Christian music festival that draws about 20,000 people. It is held on the Laguna Sega

Raceway, and I had the honor to conduct a Kidz Blitz Live event there. Hundreds of families attended KBL in a massive tent.

Have you ever talked with someone who had only one thought they wanted to convey? That was her. I mentioned that I thought it was cool to get to hang around some of the Christian music artists such as The Newsboys and Skillet. She wasn't interested in talking about the musical artists. I could see she didn't come to reminisce about the music festival. She was focused on something else.

She looked at me straight in the eye and told me something I will never forget. She said that when she and her son attended the festival 10 years ago. They knew nothing about God and had never been to church. Someone invited them, and they ended up in the massive tent where Kidz Blitz was on stage.

What she said next made my whole trip to the conference worth every mile and all the frustration.

She told me that she and her son responded to the invitation to receive Jesus and they have not been the same. She said they joined a church where they have been serving ever since. Her son, who was 8 when he accepted Jesus at Kidz Blitz, was now 18 and faithfully serving the Lord in their church. She had waited on me until all the people cleared out…to say, "thank you."

I cried.

The Calling

I am a minister. I minister to the largest mission field in the world.
I minister to children.

My calling is sure. My challenge is big. My vision is clear.
My desire is strong. My influence is eternal. My impact is critical.
My values are solid. My faith is tough. My mission is urgent.
My purpose is unmistakable. My direction is forward. My heart is genuine.
My strength is supernatural. My reward is promised.
And my God is real.

In a world of cynicism, I offer hope.
In a world of confusion, I offer truth.
In a world of immorality, I offer values.
In a world of neglect, I offer attention. In a world of abuse, I offer safety. In a world of ridicule, I offer affirmation.
In a world of division, I offer reconciliation.
In a world of bitterness, I offer forgiveness.
In a world of sin, I offer salvation. In a world of hate, I offer God's love.

I refuse to be dismayed, disengaged, disgruntled, discouraged or distracted.
Neither will I look back, stand back, fall back, go back or sit back.
I do not need applause, flattery, adulation, prestige, stature or veneration.
I do not have time for business as usual, mediocre standards, small thinking, outdated methods, normal expectations, average results, ordinary ideas, petty disputes or low vision.

I will not give up, give in, bail out, lie down, turn over, quit or surrender.
I will pray when things look bad. I will pray when things look good.
I will move forward when others stand still.
I will trust God when obstacles arise.
I will work when the task is overwhelming.
I will get up when I fall down.

My calling is to reach boys and girls for God.
It is too serious to be taken lightly, too urgent to be postponed, too vital to be ignored, too relevant to be overlooked,
too significant to be trivialized, too eternal to be fleeting and too passionate to be quenched.

I know my mission. I know my challenge.
I also know my limitations, my weaknesses, my fears and my problems.
And I know my God.

Let others get the praise. Let the church get the blessing. Let God get the glory. I am a minister. I minister to children. This is who I am. This is what I do.

Live Events

watch the video at
family-experience.com

watch the video at
kidzblitz.com

Bible Curriculum

shop online at
kidzblitzcurriculum.com

Stay in Touch!

Have you jumped a track?

Tell us about it at JumpingTheTrack.com

Keep Up With Roger

Follow me on Twitter: rogerfields
Friend me on Facebook: rogerthomasfields
RogerFields.com

Keep Up With Blitz Ministries

KidzBlitz.com

Family-Experience.com

KidzBlitzCurriculum.com

Blitz Ministries

5028 Ashgrove Road

Nicholasville, Kentucky 40356

Tel. 859.971.0019

Fax 859.264.1673

Info@kidzblitz.com

CPSIA information can be obtained at www.ICGtesting.com
Printed in the USA
LVOW070335281211

261314LV00002B/1/P